MOTHERING
WITH PURPOSE
Devotional

MOTHERING
WITH PURPOSE

Devotional

90 DAYS OF ENCOURAGEMENT FOR
MOMS ON MISSION WITH JESUS

SARA DAIGLE

Good Books

New York, New York

Good Books books may be purchased in bulk at special discounts for sales promotion, corporate gifts, fund-raising, or educational purposes. Special editions can also be created to specifications. For details, contact the Special Sales Department, Good Books, 307 West 36th Street, 11th Floor, New York, NY 10018 or info@skyhorsepublishing.com.

Good Books is an imprint of Skyhorse Publishing, Inc.®, a Delaware corporation.

Visit our website at www.goodbooks.com

10 9 8 7 6 5 4 3 2 1

Library of Congress Cataloging-in-Publication Data is available on file.

Cover art courtesy of Shutterstock.com
Cover design by Mumtaz Mustafa

Print ISBN: 978-1-68099-712-5
eBook ISBN: 978-1-68099-796-5

Printed in the United States of America

Dedicated to my own dear mother who raised ten children with fascinating grace—*all of whom call her FRIEND.*

PREFACE

B eing a third-born child in a family of ten children had me well acquainted with taking care of babies, and I entered the mothering world eagerly. There was little adjustment to having my own babies because I had helped my mother take care of my younger siblings for as long as I could remember.

I was going to do just what she did: homeschool, always be a stay-at-home mom, and be my daughters' best friends even in their teen years.

I drove an old minivan so I could afford to be a stay-at-home mother. I homeschooled and embraced the whole bake-your-own-everything kind of lifestyle. And I loved my children like none other.

Then, my world fell apart. The years of doing everything "right" had to be replaced for a trust in the only One who is always right.

My husband's choices led him away from our home and into a romantic relationship with a young girl whom we all considered a friend to our family. There are no words for the strain this placed on my children, nor for the aftermath of devastation on all our lives.

I went to work and the children went to public school. They reeled, I struggled—but we survived, and we learned, and we knew that, though life can be altered by another, it can never be destroyed by another.

In the past three years I've told my children many times over, "No one can ruin your life except you. You have the strength to get back up and live a beautiful life."

I held them when they cried, faced their deep hurt and anger when it erupted, and all of us spent many hours in therapy sessions.

After a few years of struggle, I made a move from the west coast to the east, landing in the dead of night in a major airport with myself and the children to start life over. We moved to an area where we knew one other family, settled into a house we had never seen, and started searching Google for maps to the closest schools and grocery stores. COVID-19 hit right afterward, and the rest is history.

Along with my children, I struggled to survive until Jesus set me free from the grief that would have destroyed me.

There, I learned all about grace.

There, I learned that Jesus wants to be trusted more than we trust certain methods.

There, my eyes opened wide to the fact that God was moving in all kinds of places and people—*and that the answers are not the same for every mother.*

Homeschool was no longer an idol.

I bought food rather than made it.

And Jesus became altogether lovely in the face of tragedy.

Regardless of your circumstance, I invite you to gaze with me into the face of Jesus Christ, Who alone can restore your heart while you drive the children to school, or wait with them for the bus, or teach them at your kitchen table.

Jesus wants to be *everything* for us mothers.

Parts of this book were written while I was in one world, and parts of it written while I was in another. Jesus Christ met me in both. He steadied me in both. He taught me that grief and gratitude are friends, interlaced, working together with one purpose—*to behold the Lamb of*

God who takes away the sin of the world and overcomes the effects of it, as well.

And He comes to each of you, inviting you to incredible peace in a life not your own. The Son of Man will always rise over everything that goes down.

It remains then, that your greatest need as a mother is not a perfect method, but a deep understanding of a Perfect Master.

As Eric Gilmour so beautifully says, "Jesus Christ is greater than His gifts, more wonderful than His wonders, and more precious than His promises."

All is grace.

Love always,
Sara

INTRODUCTION

"Watch your step, Mama!"

I look ahead to this man-child of mine, the one with broad shoulders holding a head mature for his age. They call him an "old soul."

He makes me happy. And today, as I follow him down the slippery dock coated in green wetness, he warns me not to slip. He could have warned his sister, but he thought mostly of his mama.

In our days jam-packed with small things, we get to carry the greatest meaning of love our kids will ever know apart from their Savior. God uses the love of a mother to describe His love for His children.

I love watching big, burly, bearded men cry over their mamas. They're so tough, so strong . . . but the thought of Mama still makes them tear up.

A few years later this same child is talking even bigger. "Mom, if we were in danger I would shoot the bad guy, throw you on my shoulders, and carry you away to safety. Also, I'd shoot deer for our food. I'd take care of all of us."

I look at him, taller than his mama now, and realize he would do exactly as he said. But then comes the punch line, "In a case like that, I'd actually be your boss, Mom!"

I smile, and agree with him. I'd listen if he knew what to do and I didn't.

Mothering four children takes every ounce of strength I have, yet allows me to love with capacity I didn't know existed before I became a mom. Daily, there's a twist and turn of events that need wisdom. This book is meant to spur us on in knowing just how much a mother means to her children and how much responsibility we have in raising them.

As my friend Kate says, "We cannot afford to absorb lies no matter how comfortably they rest on our shoulders."

Our character as mothers affirms in its private life what we proclaim in our public speech. *The call for today is that we become aware of and fully embrace our impact for tomorrow.*

Your son will very quickly say, "Watch your step, Mama!" but it is up to you to help him watch his own steps as long as he is a child. This is done in the silliness of laughter, quietness of teaching moments, and in every aspect of the crazy lives we live.

As an Amish girl raised in a family of ten children, I remember when I became aware that not all girls loved their mother like I did, that there were some girls who didn't call their mom their best friend. That realization made me even more appreciative of what I had with my mother, and even more determined to have that with my own children someday.

I watched mothers for years before I had my own four children. Each time I gave birth, I determined that this child would come before work, hobbies, or friends. My children are far from perfect, but just the other day my daughter said the same thing I had said so many years earlier. "Mama, I'm realizing that so many girls don't talk with their moms about deeper issues, and they don't like hanging out with their moms."

My mother didn't believe that love accepts all things; she believed that love changes all things. We loved her not because she made life easy on us, but because she walked with us through the hard things in life. My mother led us to the Master more than she pushed us with her method. She never depended on her own ways of doing things but helped us see we all needed Jesus in a deeply personal way. That didn't mean she ditched all rules or discipline. It did mean she loved Jesus more than she loved herself, *and we could all tell.*

I watched my grandma and aunties, realizing they were the same as my own mother. They talked about everything, laughed, played, and considered their children some of their best friends. It didn't take long for me to realize how incredibly fortunate I was. From these exemplary women, I gleaned and tried to re-create for my own children what they had given me.

The twenty-first century may be the most difficult era in which mothers have ever raised children. I want us all to be fully assured that while perfection is impossible, we still have a mandate from heaven to point our children toward a trust-walk with the God of heaven. I also want us to embrace the struggle. ***A mandate from heaven will be met with a battle from hell.***

When your child is in the midst of a violent and lengthy struggle, rather than go under with the struggle, pull upward in the battle. There, heaven will meet your soul. Let all your parenting be marked with trust. Hear me on this—you are not a terrible mother just because your child is going through a terrible struggle. Allow Jesus to walk elbow to elbow with you through it, just as He does with all others who call on Him for grace and help. The best thing love can do is willingly walk rough places with the ones we love most.

One of the best things my mother did for me was say, "I'm sorry." The memory of taking a walk with her through the woods and hearing her say, "I'm sorry I snapped at you children today," is forever seared in my mind. Today, I do the same with my own. A sincere "I'm sorry" can clear the atmosphere and have a child sit on your bed at night talking his heart out because he knows that Mama knows she isn't perfect, either. Never be afraid of owning your mistakes. The truth of all things will set your heart free, even the truth of your own failures.

You were never called to display your mothering; you were called to fully mother your children with one thing marking each move—LOVE. Jesus Christ showed me His love more clearly through my own children's struggles than He had ever shown me before. I learned what brokenness looked like, what love looked like, and what it meant to willingly embrace where we were at so we could get to a better place. I learned to work with what was before me rather than force what I wanted through fear and control. I learned to support and walk alongside them through seasons of struggle and trial. There, I learned what Grace truly meant for both me and my children.

Grace was always meant to be embraced by those who saw their need of it.

From one mother to another, may peace be the essence flowing from your soul as you read these pages and gain new courage for each trial and victory ahead.

This book is not a comprehensive how-to book on parenting (I'm far too young and inexperienced for that); rather, it is full of inspirations given to me during the last several years by the One who parents best of all—Jesus Christ. It is the honest heart of a mother who knows both struggle and victory in various stages of life. I invite you to walk with me through both.

May the knowledge that you are not alone equip and empower you as you know trust in your very bones and marrow.

"As your days, so shall your strength be" (Deuteronomy 33:25, ESV).

MOTHERING
WITH PURPOSE
Devotional

Day 1

But seek first the kingdom of God and his righteousness and all these things will be added to you." (Matthew 6:33, ESV)

It's morning, and the day begins quietly except for the *knock, knock, knock* on my office door.

I've been hiding in here with a cup of coffee, my Bible, and Jesus. Life has been so full that I'm forced to slow down just to clear my head and see what God has to say.

This morning, the knock is persistent.

"Yes, son?"

"I'm so hungry. Can I make some breakfast?"

He's too young to cook, so I ask him to wait, but I give him a snack and then get lost in my musings the second he disappears.

Knock, knock, knock—*again.*

"May I have peanut butter on my apple?"

Already my mind is swarming with what needs to be done and all the things that will happen whether or not anything on my list gets accomplished. I will load the car with kids and take them swimming, then return in time to host a houseful of guests. This morning I choose whether to start with laundry, cooking, or cleaning, but I hope all three will get done before we leave.

The kids will have a list with chores to accomplish before the fun begins, and I will be buzzing about, trying to get the house ready and food prepared.

And then, it hits me. I did this yesterday, and the day before, and the day before that. I did this last year, and the year before, and the year before that.

The floor never stays clean, and the garage refills with recycling and garbage. No one really knows how hard I work, and no one really cares that the yard is spotless.

What they remember, and what I will remember in years to come, are things of the heart. I'll say, "Remember the year we learned to spend more time together?" Or, "Remember the year we all learned to apologize?" Maybe even, "Remember the summer we spent all those evenings sitting in the living room talking about life, the importance of a relationship with Jesus, and how to have one?"

I look back to years when the kids were tiny tots and wish I had worried less about having a spotless home and focused more on sharing love in every possible way.

Mothers and wives, the rush of today will never fill our quest for the meaning of tomorrow.

The moments we give to God will bring us to the eternity we get to spend with God. Moments with God don't have to be alone, quiet, with lightly sweetened coffee and a Bible. Moments with God can be all moments in the day.

Because when God is first, the page of your day won't merely be filled with pursuits for present gratification. When you walk with God, you are quick to deny your small desires for a greater good.

You look ahead and you look behind, and you determine how today will make your goals for tomorrow become reality.

When you're sitting in that chair with a graying head, pondering life and how you lived it, you won't be sorry you paused the rush to grab a Bible and show your kids the way. You'll be truly glad you stewarded the gifts God gave you, rather than rushed through life ignoring His hand pressing your heart to be, do, and dare.

When you hear of your kids' grown-up lives, you'll be glad you took time for them—because now, you would love them to take time for you.

And as you sit, with the presence of Christ satisfying even your later years, you'll be so glad you allowed Him to remove the clutter from your page, align the words correctly, and leave a clear margin at the side.

Let little boys knock on your door repeatedly for peanut butter, and let your brain begin to swirl with a hundred demands on your day. Then, take a deep breath and remember the most important things, the things you will remember in the years ahead.

Give your moments to eternity, for in a short time, eternity will have overtaken even the comprehension of this moment in time.

Live well, for in a short blip, when time as it is ends, you will know the meaning of being fully alive. Jesus wants *that life* to permeate us now and only to continue, then.

Let eternity begin in your heart today—then, bring eternity to the hearts of all those around you.

Lord Jesus, thank You that my own quest for meaning is fulfilled in You alone. Thank You that You meet me each day whether or not I have time alone, and that Your constant presence shows itself strong to my children.

DAY 2

Jesus answered him, "If anyone loves me, he will keep my word, and my Father will love him, and we will come to him and make our home with him." (John 14:23, ESV)

It was Mother's Day as we hopped onto our bikes and hit the road, my lovely eight-year-old daughter and I.

She lagged behind and begged to bike an alternate route, while I pedaled ahead, committed to sticking to the loop we'd planned. She pouted for miles, it seemed.

Really, on Mother's Day, I thought, when I'd carved out time just for her?

As we neared town, she softened and suggested we head to the bench outside the store for a chat. It was then that I paused, and whispered in her ear a thought that had been sticking with me for the entire ride.

In the middle of the parking lot, I whispered, "What if we bike up to the carnival and I buy you some rides?"

Sparkle!

Her eyes lit up and suddenly her legs were stronger than strong. She flew along behind me, chattering happily. In no time, we were at the field where the rides stood in colorful array against a cloudy sky.

Her little-girl joy was such a delight to my heart that day. And when I told her that I had been thinking of taking her all along, her countenance dropped into a sheepishly thoughtful look. She hadn't known, or she never would have pouted for so long. She would never have lagged behind, refusing to ride beside me, had she known the fun I was thinking of giving her with my own birthday spending money.

How many times are we just like my little girl? We lag behind, grumble, and inwardly fight what's ahead because we don't see the blessing of it. If, instead, we pushed hard when the going got tough, we'd be able to ride beside our Leader and enjoy His friendship right through the tough ride. We'd be at His side, in full fellowship. We'd be talking, and hearing His heart. We'd trust when we didn't know. We'd love and be loved.

Get this—we'd never feel alone. Loneliness is one of the worst experiences for human hearts. If only we saw that our lagging keeps us alone, *but our willingness to push hard after Him keeps us in the Company we need most of all.* We need His Presence more than we need the hard things removed. Staying beside Him, we'd actually have grace, and lots of it—not just when it's easy, but right through the tough times.

It's never OK, like my daughter did, to lag behind Christ and spit out ugliness to those around us. Rather, we need to get beside Jesus. He either wants to remove the hard from your life or He wants to ride right beside you.

When you hold His hand through the hard, you may well find more growth and blessing than if there had been no hard at all.

Teach your kids to follow you before they understand, so they can follow Christ later. Be faithful to lead them to good places when you ask them to push somewhere.

Never allow your child to push without bringing them to blessing. Reward them, so they can see the results of their labor. Talk to them about life, Christ, and the blessing of following through when the way is tough. There may not be a carnival, but let their hearts know blessing at the end of the ride.

Nick Vujicic's parents didn't know the glory of their son's ride when he was born without arms or legs, but they parented him so well that he was happier than many kids who have every limb intact. What he didn't have in arms and legs, he had in joy. I couldn't keep from staring at his eyes when I flipped through his book, subtitled *Inspiration for Living a Ridiculously Good Life.* His eyes—they were powerful, strong, and alive. My own welled in tears as I saw him "standing" in front of crowds and loving on the hurting.

So often, I see the opposite. Worn faces and weathered expressions, faces dead while bodies stand in perfectly good condition.

It's not what our journey is made of, but what we make of our journey. Show your kids Mr. Vujicic's life. Tell them how he weathered the ride and came to a blessed end. Most of all, tell them they can, too.

Teach them to ride beside you in obedience, then lead them to walk beside Christ.

Father, help us show our children what obedience looks like. Help us follow You through thick and thin, then lead our children to do the same. Thank You that Your reward waits for all those who put You first.

Day 3

Go through, go through the gates, prepare the way for the people; build up, build up the highway; clear it of stones; lift up a signal over the peoples.

Behold, the Lord has proclaimed to the ends of the earth: Say to the daughter of Zion, "Behold, your salvation comes; behold, His reward is with Him, and His recompense is before Him."

And they shall be called The Holy People, The Redeemed of the Lord; and you shall be called Sought Out, A City Not Forsaken. (Isaiah 62:10–12, ESV)

I pulled up to the immaculate little spa, noting purple blooms spilling their beauty from three hanging baskets as I walked through the narrow porch.

My friend is one of those prayer warriors, and we go to her spa when we need prayer. She's safe and so loving you can trust her with those things you just don't tell people unless you already know you're safe. Her office is prepared to host a soul needing rest. Mild colors on the walls blended perfectly with lovely furniture while her décor added warmth and beauty to the room. I wanted to go home and paint every room in my house after sitting there, but I soaked hers in, instead.

How can someone look another in the eye and ask question after question without making them feel uncomfortable? And then, how can one host God's Presence so strongly that the tears flow and, after being prayed for, women rest on her cot in utter quietness and peace, entirely enveloped in God-consciousness?

For a few hours, this dear lady soaked my body in Israeli pink mud, gave me a facial, prayed over my life, then sent me home with face creams and an invitation to return in a month for another treatment free of charge.

She knows she cannot do the work, but she prepares the way for God's Spirit to do His. And, as she prepared the way for my friend and I, so we mothers are called to prepare the way for our kids.

In Isaiah chapter 10, God asks us to go through gates.

He asks us to prepare the way.

He asks us to build up the highway, and then, He asks us to go a step further and clear the road of stones.

Finally, He wants us to lift a signal over the people.

We prepare the way when we read the Bible to our kids at night. We build up the highway when we're not afraid of their tough questions regarding our faith, and we don't shrink back from openly discussing things they wonder about. We clear the road of stones when we anticipate future roadblocks to their faith and go out of our way to speak into those areas of life long before the questions rise in their own hearts. We speak up long before an atheistic college professor speaks out. We lift a signal over our kids when we bring God into our lives and establish His daily presence in our hearts and homes. When blessings come, we give verbal thanks. When trials remain, we let our kids see us on our knees. When time is scarce, we still make time for the things that are most important.

After praying in that lovely little spa, I picked up my daughter from a week of camp. She was tanned from the sun and, as happens each year, she wore a T-shirt marked with messages from her new friends. And again, she climbed into the car reluctantly because one more year of camp was over.

"Mama, we missed swim time because we were up all night, praying," she said. "And I felt God so strongly over me."

Just a week prior, I had rushed around buying her clothes and snacks during a full weekend of woodcutting at our house. It didn't seem a great time for her to be heading off to camp, because we had just moved. But something told me that these small things were preparing the way for larger things—*and it was all worth it.*

Something whispers to my heart that purchasing a gift card for my son's friend and heading to that party is more than worth it—because small things create large relationships, and this friend was one of the best for my son. Not every teenage boy will mentor my son into the best response for that bully who just belittled someone. And I'm watching this boy's mother, how she smiles at her kids and creates a warm atmosphere in her home. We laugh at our mutual love for remaking old into new with a few cans of chalk paint—but both of us know that small things like spray paint create larger things like warm home atmospheres.

Mothers, you are preparing the way.

Host Christ so you can pray over your kids like my friend prays in her spa.

Read apologetics so you have answers to your kids' tough questions regarding your faith.

Create a warm atmosphere in your home so your family will want to be there.

Talk often about the things most important to you—and make sure that the Infinite is more vital to your heart than the finite.

Christ will do His work, but He asks you to prepare the way!

Lord Jesus, fill me with vision and integrity so strongly that I cannot help but do Your work for my children. Fill me to overflowing as I read Your Word to them at night. If I preach for anyone, let me preach first to my children.

DAY 4

Therefore encourage one another and build one another up, just as you are doing." (1 Thessalonians 5:11, ESV)

"You're watching a movie together?" I asked my little boy. He nodded his head while big sister sat on the couch scrolling through her phone, revealing her obvious disinterest in cartoons, but willingness to sit with him anyway—all unnoticed by him as he sat in rapt attention.

This wasn't the first time she had given an evening to her little brother's cause, and he loved her for it. I smiled at them and walked into the kitchen. "Nice kitchen!" I called out moments later as I placed a bowl of melon in the fridge and bent to pick up a few missed chocolate cake crumbs.

Then, it hit me. I could have complained that they chose a movie to watch together rather than find a game to play. I could even have turned off the TV.

Then, I could have noticed the bowl of fruit left out in the open to attract fruit flies, and I could have corrected that. I could have hollered at the next daughter to redo her sweeping job when I noticed those luscious crumbs on the floor.

And hear this—I could have even told her not to bake a two-layer chocolate cake oozing with vanilla pudding and homemade frosting. I could have told her that I was on a sugar fast and didn't want sweets around to be tortured with.

Instead, I took her to Walmart for the needed supplies and supported each turn of her endeavor. For twenty-four hours I watched her and her sister scoop massive bites of gooey goodness into their mouths while I groaned on the sidelines, deprived of all things sweet.

And when I saw her watching a movie with her little brother, I smiled in appreciation rather than criticized her choice. When I saw the fruit left out of the fridge, I quietly covered it and placed it in the fridge. When I noticed crumbs on the table, I bent to pick them up while hollering above the screen noise, "Nice kitchen!"

I did those things on purpose.

Every day, we make choices on purpose because none of it just happens. It's so much easier to snap at mistakes and focus on improving our children on all fronts than it is to shut our mouths and strive to show appreciation for everything we can.

Earlier, when I took the child to Walmart for cake-decorating supplies, I snapped at her involuntarily. The very thing I was trying to do was undone in a moment.

I stalled. What on earth was wrong with me?

I stopped immediately and said, "I just snapped at you, and I'm sorry. That was wrong."

Mothers, those are some of the best words you will ever say to your children. Mistakes are inevitable, but apologies are not optional. When your words wreck a moment, allow an apology to recreate the day. Your children will never forget your willingness to admit your own wrong.

She looked sad and I kept trying to make it up to her. She forgave me and I was able to pull her back into the conversation she was trying to have with her mama. The rest of the day I must have gotten five kisses and hugs from this child I had wounded with my words and lack of listening.

Do we see how important our words are? I'd much rather thank a child for a clean kitchen, smile at her for spending time with her brother, and take her out for some special supplies for her secret love of cake decorating, than let her know how she could improve each moment of everything she did or didn't do.

Children desperately need to feel appreciated. Mothers are trainers, yes—but we are also safety nets, encouragers, and faith builders. We are called to notice and encourage every good thing about our children. By doing this, we motivate them to more goodness.

Emotional safety can't happen in an atmosphere of constant correction and criticism. Just as we appreciate a boss who calls out all the best in us, so children flourish under care where their efforts are noticed and praised.

Because they are far from perfect, we can't afford to wait to speak out appreciation until everything is done to perfection.

Notice your child.

Appreciate your child.

Keep them in a greenhouse of appreciation rather than a desert of thirst for approval.

You want your child to feel relaxed, safe, and at ease. You don't want them to jump inwardly when they know a mistake has been made. You want them to walk through life learning as they go, all from a place of acceptance and appreciation.

Knowing God's love is the one and only thing that will truly change us. God is much more interested in His children knowing His love than He is in them cringing under His supposed rod when they make a mistake. Show your children the love of Jesus by showing them comfort and safety with you. Today, choose to use your voice for appreciation at least five times more than for criticism.

Lord Jesus, bring our hearts to peace. Thank You that there's peace in spite of all the imperfections we encounter daily as we raise our children. Sometimes we long for just one perfect thing, but life is messy and real. Help us simply be at peace and call forth all the good our children strive so hard for.

DAY 5

Be kind to one another, tenderhearted, forgiving one another, as God in Christ forgave you." (Ephesians 4:32, ESV)

We sat around the table, eating whatever struck our fancy. There were pumpkin spice drinks the nine-year-old made on a whim, topped high with whipped cream—the real, thick stuff. There was chips and salsa, and even cereal. It was Sunday night, and no one felt like cooking a real dinner.

They started talking, these four kids who hold my heart in a tight ball of love-drenched tenderness. We must have sounded like a madhouse or crazy crowd, and even I was surprised at the openness and honesty coming from their lips. At their age, I would have been embarrassed to say such things about my own heart, desires, and thoughts.

The drinks were downed in short order, but we lingered. I got a deeper glimpse into my son's heart. He trusted me enough, trusted all of us enough to be vulnerable with some of his deepest feelings. He felt relaxed; he knew he was loved, not just a little, but a whole lot.

Opinions flew around the table faster than one could absorb them, but it was OK. Because sometimes it is more important to be honest than to sound right. Sometimes it is more important to listen than to teach, and always it is vital to let our kids know how much they are loved.

I tuck the five-year-old into bed, and I whisper, "Jesus loves you so very much, and Mama does, too." I say it purposefully, often, because the child who knows he is loved has no need to hide, no need to build a shell around himself as he grows older.

They crawl all over me, asking for back rubs, hugs, and time spent together. My ten-year-old son leans forward during church services and motions for me to scratch his back. My nine-year-old daughter cuddles into my right, and together they share a chocolate drink.

Surround your kids with silly, sloppy, smiling love, and you will be able to take them from there right into Bible time, when you get to share your greatest passion.

Mothers, you are one of your kids' greatest teachers. Your words, not only your life, will be of great influence. Never hesitate to establish times of Bible reading and prayer on a daily basis, even if you are the only parent home to lead it.

Mothering should be one of our greatest motivations to find out what Jesus meant when He said, "I have told you this so that my joy may be in you and that your joy may be complete" (John 15:11 NIV).

Just as the world is turned off by religion, so your kids will be turned away from a preaching of righteousness without the love and joy they crave. Mothers, we must be indwelled by the Giver of Light if we are to lead our children to any light at all.

We must find personal, deep, satisfying communion with Christ so we can share it with them, more than a list of rules, don'ts, and "God hates that."

Though vital to every home, rules cannot be expected to be the greatest means of holding your child's heart. It's not that rules should be amiss—the happiest kids are those who know some boundaries. Homes with both love and discipline create a power-filled atmosphere that almost no child can resist. *You don't need to do everything perfectly, but you need to have perfect love.*

Perfect love knows how to be silly, smiley, firm, require respect and obedience, and love your child so well that he opens right up long before he's a teen. Perfect love requires respect, but earns it as well.

And as surely as a circle is round, so surely perfect love includes both steadfast rules and obedience right alongside silly, sloppy, smiley love.

Lord Jesus, help my kindness create a safe space for messy days and messy hearts. Help me invite my children to enjoy life with me long before everything is perfect inwardly or outwardly.

Day 6

Mercy and truth are met together; righteousness and peace have kissed each other." (Psalm 85:10, ESV)

I dropped her off in Seattle at 5:00 a.m. and whispered aloud, "God, thank you for a mother like her."

She had hugged me long before walking away. And when she walked away, somehow she stayed with me. She has more patience and grace for ten children than most have for two, and I'm watching her after many years so I can learn more of the Christ in her. My mother cares little for earthly things, but much for heavenly. After, and even during, raising her own ten kids, she'd bring in other kids who needed a home. She'd bring out the math books for those kids as well as her own, and she'd hold and nurture them at night just as she did her own.

Now that her ten are grown and most of us have left home, she's had four girls in her home from three different families. Girls who need her love and care because they've been through more trauma than girls should know at that age. She's reading books and learning all she can about helping others—and all the while she's serving her own family.

My mother knew how to turn ancient old houses into cozy homes, how to serve her family without resenting it. **She took what money she had and multiplied it with contentment.** And no matter what, she always loved, laughed, and shared her heart with ours. We spent many hours talking, walking, shopping, eating—always free to be ourselves and say what we needed to say.

A child cannot make her mother her best friend. Only a mother can make herself worthy of that name. My mother did, even through those years many call turbulent teens. Somehow she knew how to require obedience while still holding the heart. All ten of us knew beyond doubt that Mama loved our hearts no matter how icky they were, that she cried when we were sad—and when our lives were blessed she was happy enough to soar through the sky.

When we were tots, all of us knew she was in charge and had the final say. We didn't get to boss Mama around, because she knew that children in charge of their own lives bear too much weight on their shoulders—weight meant only for adults to carry. She led us to good places because we weren't wise enough to do so on our own. We learned that Mama meant what she said—and it was all said in love. I asked her the other day, "Mom, how would you train your eleven-year-old son to clean his room as I've asked him to?"

"Consequences—I just wouldn't put up with it," she replied.

I ran upstairs and followed through. I know by her example that grace and love doesn't mean permissive disobedience.

Christ's love, when fully realized, removes sin from our lives rather than condones it. *One cannot know Love without being changed by that Love.*

My mother knew that true love in her would guide us to Love Jesus truly—because isn't that what the heart was created for most of all? She knew that requiring obedience in love would ultimately enable us to know what Christ's gift of love meant.

When we're not changed by Love, we don't truly know love. If Love didn't change lives, it wouldn't be Love at all.

Love is what love is—and when you know Love, you do what love does.

Perhaps, rather than expecting love to accept all things, we need to accept that love changes all things.

Where our treasure is, there our hearts will be.

May our treasure be changeless love so we can bring it to a changing world.

Father, help us to be fully assured that Your love embodies both mercy and truth. Help us to hold our conviction with compassion as we give extravagantly to those around us.

Day 7

Every good gift and every perfect gift is from above, coming down from the Father of lights. (James 1:17, ESV)

I looked down at my son's feet, and my eyes popped much like they did the other day when he pulled me up to a mirror, flexed his muscles, and showed me how much broader his shoulders were than my own. I love that he's growing in both height and stature as well as character and conduct. I simply hadn't known how big his feet were until he pulled a few pairs of shoes off the shelf and asked if I'd buy them. Of course I said yes.

There's something almost puzzling about watching your little boy become a man. Like, when does that happen and how is it even possible?

I had taken the three oldest out for one of our clothes-shopping days because they were all popping at the seams as they sprouted taller than their mother. One thing after another landed in the cart in hopes that they'd have clothes that actually fit for a few more months.

Then there was the food. We pulled into Aldi rather than a sit-down restaurant, because who can afford both eating out and clothes shopping with such a crew? Once again the cart loaded up with food and snacks to eat in the car while opinions were tossed around freely, sometimes at the expense of another.

My sister and I laughed at the three as they lived up the moment, and I was loving it.

For years I had grocery shopped with my children, and lately I had been missing that time together as life took us in opposite directions more and more. But as life changes, it is always possible to create new ways of spending time together. It's so important to be intentional about it.

Sometimes, that means having special holiday traditions. At our house, it's setting up the Christmas tree the day after Thanksgiving. The child who loves to decorate most helps put pumpkins away and bring ornaments out. The youngest child gets to help hang them on the tree.

But then there are the regular rhythms that happen week in and week out. Like having Bible time together in the evenings whenever possible. I gather them in to read and pray before bedtime, and it opens a door for truth to shed light onto hearts that have heard and seen enough of a dark world. Sometimes we're all on my king-sized bed. Sometimes they're grouchy and tired. But it's a ritual that brings stability and belonging to their lives.

Or like making sure Little Buddy has Mama's touch before bed, perhaps a snuggle, story, kiss, talking, holding hands—or maybe all of the above. He's nine years old and too old to sleep in Mama's bed—but none of my children are too old to be hugged or even held.

Another tradition is pausing to scratch my son's back in the morning—just because it means a lot to him and it's *our thing, the thing I do to connect and show love.* Because we do this, we often have a laugh together first thing in the morning. Creating time means memories are made without even trying.

Gone are the days when they were all tiny and I'd have a cart overflowing with milk and babies. But the days will never be gone when I spend time with them.

I'm creating memories by living moments. What we can't afford to do on a two-week vacation to Hawaii we can afford to bring in a moment to our home.

I'm creating belonging by giving them family time, activities, and space to be part of.

When something good happens in a child's life over and over again, it creates a stabilizing factor for them to ground their lives to, to remember, to be influenced by.

Your children need you to reach out and make it happen.

They need to know certain good things will happen at certain times.

They need to know that busyness stops for a few minutes so that there's space for good times.

Mothers, we need this, too. When I'm less disciplined and lazy with my time, I'm frustrated internally and feel a void of what could have and should have been. Good things don't just happen.

Our ritual can be as simple as creating a list for them to do each morning. Before I leave for work, I copy chores under each child's name. Knowing they are guided whether or not I'm home helps them when I'm away. The older ones can help make sure Little Buddy does what he needs to do. His "job" is to jump on the trampoline one hundred times every day. The little fella needs to get his blood moving. I create both memories and health by creating this small and seemingly trivial "tradition" for his day.

Whether it's clothes shopping with growing teens or giving that morning back rub, find ways to create daily, weekly, and yearly traditions with your children. The effort you give will repay itself a hundredfold!

Father, thank You that You daily load us with blessings. Help us reach into those gifts and pull them to our children in special and unique ways. Help us give time and energy to creating moments with and for our children.

Day 8

And those twelve stones, which they took out of the Jordan, Joshua set up at Gilgal.

And he said to the people of Israel, "When your children ask their fathers in times to come, 'What do these stones mean?'

Then you shall let your children know, 'Israel passed over this Jordan on dry ground.'

For the Lord your God dried up the waters of the Jordan for you until you passed over, as the Lord your God did to the Red Sea, which He dried up for us until we passed over,

So that all the peoples of the earth may know that the hand of the Lord is mighty, that you may fear the Lord your God forever." (Joshua 4:20–24, ESV)

I didn't expect to turn upside down when I tumbled out of an airplane two miles in the air.

I gasped for air, twisted and turned, and finally "landed" on my stomach as my body kept hurling itself toward the ground. The free fall was so exhilarating I almost didn't think about how I'd land without breaking my legs.

The process, more than the landing, was the joy of the experience. I didn't sky-dive so I could land—I did it so I could *fly.*

We often push through life as if the destination was the only thing to be concerned about, but life is all about process. Moments are what make an hour, hours are what make a day, days are what make a year.

I want to encourage us mothers to embrace whatever process we're in, whether it's simply getting up and cooking breakfast, whether it's potty training for two weeks (or more), or whether it's a rough season in much greater areas.

God is interested in each part of the journey, and He uses all of it to lead us to our destination.

None of us mothers get to escape trials, but all of us get to access an aspect of God's character that makes all things possible. This means even our very difficult trials can be graced with promised peace and joy.

Rather than live out of human shortage, we can live out of God's abundance.

God never said to expect an easy life, but He did promise an easy yoke and a light burden. Understanding this difference is a key element in emotional and spiritual maturity for us mothers, one that will affect our children more than we are aware.

The spirit in a home affects small children long before they can speak and reason. Even a baby is affected by the atmosphere into which they are born. The Spirit alive within you is one of the greatest causes for your children to hope for salvation and blessing. They will see, feel, and know true love long before they are even aware of what it is.

Mothers, don't be afraid of the difficult things in your life. If they were not there, would there ever be a need to part waters and allow God to work wonders as only He can do?

Your children need your testimony. They won't stand in awe of God's grace in your life if all seems ease and sunshine, but they will when they know the obstacles you overcame.

"And they overcame them by the blood of the Lamb, and by the word of their testimony, and they loved not their lives unto the death" (Revelation 12:11, KJV).

Not only you, but your children also, will overcome by the blood of the Lamb and by the word of your testimony. ***Don't be afraid; lean into the hard, for in doing so you will lean right into grace and allow your child to see it.*** You are the greatest avenue for showing wholeness to your children as they live in a fragmented world.

There is nothing impassable when Christ leads you. Be willing to walk *through* it so your children can see Christ *in* it.

Today, whatever is going on in your life, know that the process is just as important as the outcome, the journey is as meaningful as the destination, and nothing is ever wasted with God.

Free-fall right into your moments today, *let yourself fly*, and inhale the air Christ gives you just as you need it for each day of grace. Your life may be messy, but grace wins.

Father, thank You for wanting us to depend on You for life, joy, and peace. Thank You for these gifts stronger than any circumstance we face. Thank You that each moment of our journey is meaningful with You, and matters just as much as the destination. Help us to show the wholeness of Your grace to our children as they live in a fragmented world.

DAY 9

Finally, brothers, whatever is true, whatever is honorable, whatever is just, whatever is pure, whatever is lovely, whatever is commendable, if there is any excellence, if there is anything worthy of praise, think about these things. (Philippians 4:8, ESV)

It was nearing Christmastime, and I didn't want it to be all about Santa. All year, many kids are told to be behave or Santa won't come with their favorite toys. What's more, they've been told to put their teeth under their pillow so the tooth fairy can replace them with money. Sooner or later, they grow up and realize Mama or Daddy placed money under the pillow, and Santa never, ever came down the chimney. They realize with a twinge of "something" that Mama warning them to be good or else Santa wouldn't come was her way of gaining behavioral compliance. Years of anticipation, trust, and belief melt down to nothing, while *we adults expect the truth to transfer beautifully into biased little minds with no undesired repercussions.*

What about trust, and being able to believe Mama and Daddy? What about the fight for faith when they're older and everything clamors for their disbelief rather than faith?

At our house, we play pretend games. But I never, ever lie to the kids about make-believe. My five-year-old may love Santa, but he will never be told Santa is real and will visit the house in the night with all kinds of goodies. He'll watch the growing pile of gifts under the tree and feel loved by Mama while she reads a make-believe story of Santa. *Imagination is fun; lies are not.*

We may watch a Christmas movie with sleigh bells and reindeer, but all the kids know this is a kind of pretend fun, just a bit like their own make-believe games. There is no trust to regain after they find out the truth from childhood fantasy based on lies. There is no false hope dashed to pieces when they realize they need to ask Mama, not Santa, for what they want, *just like they ask for everything else.*

I don't want to laugh at my kids when they find out the truth, nor do I want to cringe. I don't want to play with their unbiased, implicit trust birthed from a fresh, unadulterated mind waiting to be filled *with something.*

Indulge the wonder of your child with fascinating grace! Feed his curiosity with Bible miracles and stories, and even with imaginative, make-believe characters and movies. Just don't lie to your child.

My little boy begs for Bible cartoon stories and is deeply fascinated with what he's learning. At night he begs for Old Testament stories on creation, kings, war, and peace. His name is David, and he loves reading about King David's adventures! I sit on his bed at night and we read, talk, and snuggle as we learn all about true stories that blow us away. The next morning his "quiet time" will consist of more cartoon Bible stories, and the combination drives it home. He loves both because both satisfy his need for stories with wild adventure and imagination, bravery, love, war, hate, and peace.

There are so many ways to satisfy the curiosity of your child! Make him curious about God by saturating his environment with engaging stories of God's works. Make him curious about faith by reading to him about King David's faith when he faced off giant Goliath and cut his head off.

Your young child's eyes will pop with those stories, and his heart will expand while his soul deepens. It's the perfect way to end a day, and all of it is truth.

Make sure there is less room in his heart to doubt instead of adding to the thousand reasons the devil will throw his way when he's older.

Father, give me wisdom on how to create joy and imagination for my children without feeding them lies. Help me to win trust at an early age by giving them a solid understanding of reality.

Day 10

So God created man in His own image; in the image of God He created him, male and female He created them. (Genesis 1:27, ESV)

Let your child know the truth—that he was created by God, in the image of God, for the glory of God.

God created animals, but when He created man and woman, they were specifically designed in the image of God. The difference between being created in the image of God or evolving from an amoeba is huge.

The former restores both dignity and meaning to the human race in preparation for a Christ-filled eternity. The latter allows your kids to live like hell with no thought of heaven before them.

Create your own imaginative tales and enjoy those of others, but even more, delve into true, real, and life-giving stories. **Refuse to allow Disney magic to replace the God-miraculous.**

In all reality, those God miracles trump Cinderella's imaginary glass shoe and a nonexistent tooth fairy. One captures the minds of our children but isn't real at all; the other captures the hearts of our children and is the essence of all reality.

God's miracles changed lives *for real.*

Even Disney can't compare to the wonder God gives in stories of His engagement with His people or His creation of them.

If you have a difficult time engaging the questions of your growing child, begin listening to apologists and creationists such as Norman Geisler or Ken Ham. Countless times I've turned on the podcasts on my phone as I scrubbed the bathroom, learning about Christ in ways I wanted to be able to teach my children.

Learn how to love Christ, host His presence, defend His truth, and hold Him out to your kids as the Creator He truly is. ***We are meant to shape culture more than allow it to shape us.***

Lord Jesus, thank You for creating us in Your image so You could have a relationship with us. Help us to transfer this wonder to our children. Help us to be aware of truth so we can know how to explain things to our children before doubt settles in.

Day 11

O Lord, you are my God; I will exalt you; I will praise your name, for you have done wonderful things, plans formed of old, faithful and sure. (Isaiah 25:1, ESV)

The day begins with the five-year-old running downstairs, upset at the barking dog. That dog.

It ends with the five-year-old running downstairs again, this time sobbing his little heart out as he trudges to the bathroom. I smell it, then, that strong odor that makes every mama cringe. His little pants were full and he was distraught.

As I scrubbed him with warm, soapy water and clothed him in his warmest pajamas, I wondered how a mama could love more. Here he was, interrupting my quiet time after a full day with smelly underwear and loud tears, wailing in the shower as I scrubbed him down . . . and my heart was full.

How is a full heart in that scenario possible?

I got to help him. I got to wash his little face and see a fresh spark when we were through. Then, I got to wrap him up snugly and rock him to near sleep with songs of the Jesus who loves us both.

Speaking of Savior love, it was only this morning that I got to sit under the sweetest worship while the kids played. We got intimately close to the heart of Christ and we worshipped with such abandon I felt near heaven.

The people of Christ were warm, loving, and kind, and Christ is even kinder, sweeter, more loving. I *was swept away.*

I call those early Sunday mornings my candy for the week. It's here, when those seriously in love with Christ gather to discover more of His heart and to worship with most abandon.

During worship, I look over to my friend nearby, holding her baby close. She shouts it out, this worship and excitement over love greater even than she has for her own children. We're both thrilled with Jesus, that His love meets us each day with a Presence we can't deny and wouldn't want to live without. We both need love greater than the love we give to these little ones.

Mothers need love.

Mothers need grace.

Mothers need the "high" of worship in abandon to the Christ who will never abandon us.

We really can't do this on our own. But then, we weren't meant to. Because just as I love to hold and comfort my little son in his utter nighttime distress, so Christ loves to hold me.

I'm honored He should use a mother's love to describe His own love for His children. He loves to wash me clean? Loves to wipe my tears, loves to make my heart peacefully quiet?

Just as my son needed me, so I need Christ.

And just as I loved to take my son in all his smelly mess, so Christ loves to take me in all of mine.

We're all children, really. Children of the most loving Father ever in the messiest moments of our lives.

Mothers need Him. Mothers get to find Him, then show Him off to their children!

Jesus, thank You that, though we are taken with our children each day, You invite us to be so taken with Yourself that we get lost in Who You are.

Day 12

Behold, children are a heritage from the Lord, the fruit of the womb a reward." (Psalm 127:3, ESV)

Crunching on a pine cone with my snow-laden boot brings me back to childhood with such nostalgia I can only lift my nose to the sky and take it all in.

Not every child was as fortunate as I was. Stellar Dad, empathetic mother. And I wake this morning asking myself, "What do the children need today?" Because sometimes, what the kids need and what I want are two very different things.

Like yesterday, when the eleven-year-old asked if he could stop by Walmart, and I said yes. He had a list, this growing son of mine, and it took him a while to find new socks, work gloves, and pellets for his gun. I'm standing in the aisle waiting for him to appear, my arms laden with milk jugs.

His bill equals thirty dollars and I'm getting just a wee bit grouchy by now. Sundays aren't meant for Walmart lists, I tell him. Next time could he wait for a shopping day?

"But I've been waiting for days," he said, and I knew it was true.

This morning when the snow falls I resist the urge to accomplish, and I let them play. We make hot chocolate and toast for breakfast, and before long I have four rosy-cheeked, happy kids surrounding me. "I love snow days!" the five-year-old declares. "I'm so impressed!"

I sled the hills with them, and we throw snowballs around. The world is white and friends have us over to share the joy of their hills. Black cows stand in stark contrasted colors with green hay and white snow, and we're living the moments of our best lives.

Do we miss the best in our rush for the good? Like when I'm standing in the kitchen on my phone, ready to read a mommy blog when I should be in the moment, actually *being a mommy?*

Or when I push them through so many academics that they are stressed more than saturated?

Are we so busy capturing the moments on our phones that we end up not living the moments? Do we know our kids would rather have us smile with them and at them, than have us stand before them asking them to smile *one more time* for a photo we can display?

Perhaps moments don't need to be captured as much as they need to be lived.

When we have a choice, our feelings or the good of our kids, what will we choose? Are we able to lead them in righteousness because we also know how to walk in the good and best? Can we lay aside our wants for their needs?

Sacrificing your desires for their good, mothers, bring rich dividends not to be compared with any temporary ease.

It may be easier to feed your child junk foods; go out of your way to establish his health instead.

It will be easier to sit him in front of the screen while you cook dinner; let him pull up a chair and help you cut veggies for a salad, instead.

It will be faster to hush his crying, stop the flow of tears, and move on; take time to talk him through his feelings and help him decide what the solution is.

Take time, mothers. Time cannot be bought—it can only be shared and given.

We are called to make everyday choices for eternal blessing. Sharing Christ's presence and love with our kids is the single most imperative thing we will ever do.

Sharing Christ with your kids begins by sharing yourself with your kids. Kids won't be drawn to your Savior if they haven't been drawn close to your heart.

Father, help me to invest time and energy into my children.
Thank You for this heritage from You, for this reward from You.
Help me to honor them as such.

Day 13

Not that I am speaking of being in need, for I have learned in whatever situation I am to be content. I know how to be brought low, and I know how to abound. In any and every circumstance, I have learned the secret of facing plenty and hunger, abundance and need. I can do all things through him who strengthens me. (Philippians 4:11–13, ESV)

I scrubbed furiously that week, ecstatic at purchasing a house for the first time ever.

The kitchen was a dream, and the house, though nothing fancy, was larger than I dared hope for. It had three bathrooms and a multitude of bedrooms, a sun porch and hot tub, and even a sauna downstairs.

For many years I had waited to call a house my own. With renting, I was accustomed to cleaning up other people's mess, creating a home—and then, leaving.

I lived in a two-bedroom apartment for four years, crowded so tightly things fell out of the closet when I opened the door. Then there was the old farmhouse. It was old and paneled with dark walls, and the outside desperately needed a makeover. Next was a small green house on the bay. It had a beautiful view but no storage, and I bumped my head often as I crouched under the house in search of stored items. Rats infested the area and chewed into many of our things, including plastic food buckets. But the view made up for lack of space, and once again I created a home out of the house. The yard brightened up with flowers better than ever right before I left once again, this time to my own home.

It took my breath away the first time I saw it, and I fell in love. One walk through the house made me feel as if I had known the place forever.

Having a house of my own felt like a dream. And as I scrubbed those walls, I felt a little dazed. After all these years, me, in a place like this? How would I tell friends who also longed to own a home? How could I tell them that I, too, lived for many years struggling for money and living in less-than-perfect houses that weren't my own?

I felt a little reluctant to be this happy if others were still working hard for the same goals. I wanted them to know that I had struggled, too—and all this was a surprise gift, unexpected and undeserved.

That day, I keenly felt the truth that things don't bring ultimate joy. I had been given much joy in run-down houses and cramped apartments. It didn't take a large home to create a large love.

But did I know how to abound as well? Or did I somehow think that goodness and love always meant sacrifice?

My friend, the motherly friend who always sat me down to tea and homemade cookies when I stopped by, leaned toward me as she said, "I have a verse for you! 'The blessing of the Lord makes rich, and He adds no sorrow with it'" (Proverbs 10:22, ESV).

See this? Paul knew how to have little, or much. And I, accustomed to little, was now learning to receive much, all the while learning that having more was not the source to ultimate joy.

The friend in a mud hut may have more joy than the girl in a mansion. The secret is not having much in possession, but in possessing much joy. This is why those small houses could host warmth and love just as well as this larger one.

Always strive to create something out of nothing, to make much out of little, and to use creative energy when the pocketbook is lean.

Strive to change the atmosphere for the better wherever you are. Strive to be content whether you have much or little, so that you can be blessed in less, or more.

Let's teach our children the joys of faithfulness, hard work, and contentment more than the temporal happiness that comes when they get what they want. Let's do this by example!

Strive to love, to know riches through love. Because when you do, life will bring riches your way whether you are in an old kitchen or a great big remodeled one exceeding your dreams.

The kitchen won't bring the joy as much as the pattern of love in your life will bring joy. Scrub an old one, or new—but follow hard after joy!

Lord Jesus, help us mothers to be content with less than the beauty we see on Pinterest. Help us not always be striving for the best in material things, but strive more to bring perfect eternal things to our children.

Day 14

But the path of the righteous is like the light of dawn, which shines brighter and brighter until full day. (Proverbs 4:18, ESV)

It was such a full summer. I loved settling into our new home and accomplishing little fix-up jobs before school began. But nothing takes the place of love, and one day I felt acute frustration with clean floors because I wanted clean hearts more—and it wasn't happening.

We may rush about and acquire all the outward beauty we love, and then miss out on true beauty while the things we worked hard for begin to rust away. We can burn ourselves out striving for more, more, and more material possessions or outward beauty when our children won't remember either one as much as they will remember our inner beauty reflected in both our countenance and the atmosphere created in our homes.

Everything we work for on this planet begins to erode slowly the moment it is finished. But everything we experience in Christ—all the love, joy, and peace—multiplies through eternity. This is why a home with love and laughter will be remembered while an immaculate home devoid of those things will bring a sting to those whose memory it occupies.

This week I sat with two other moms, discussing the school year ahead of us. We all wanted to begin a writing club for our kids, and I drove home wondering if I could pull it off with the love and peace I desire in our home. Would the hours spent critiquing papers for this little club become the last straw in the day? I rose the next morning, realizing I'd probably need to decline. Because good things, as well as bad things, can take the peace from our lives.

Our souls were never meant to perform well on the zip line. We need the walk more than the zip. And if we're constantly on the zip line we bypass the walk while our lips form talk our kids have no evidence for.

Mothers and wives, we may ask ourselves: *are our paths shining?* Our countenance can't be shining if our brow is always creasing. If you are always at the end of your rope gasping for air, how will you share your oxygen with those around you? If I have no time to refresh myself, how will I refresh another? I can only give what I possess.

I'd rather have a smaller home than a large one full of unhappy people. I'd rather never vacation in an RV than take a trip where each person is brittle and exhausted.

Because soul things, not material things, make up this beautiful life thing. And when soul things are in place, we get to truly love and enjoy the material blessings that come our way.

Enjoy your home, because it is a gift from God. But enjoy Him first, and keep His love first in your heart.

Keep your soul beautiful first of all, and God will add to your life everything He sees you truly need.

Lord Jesus, thank You for promising a path that shines more and more. Fill us with Your Spirit so this is what we bring to our children's atmosphere. Help them see us following hard after meaningful, beautiful lives.

DAY 15

Thus says the Lord: 'Stand by the roads, and look, and ask for the ancient paths, where the good way is; and walk in it, and find rest for your souls. But they said, 'We will not walk in it.'' (Jeremiah 6:16, ESV)

My alarm went off at 6:00 a.m., as usual, and I quickly shampooed my hair before walking into the kitchen for my early morning kombucha.

I used to think the drink was gross, but wisdom has it that fermented things are better for us than most other things we eat. I've become accustomed to its sour tang and appreciate the probiotics washing down any nasty cells that may or may not be accumulating.

I opened the door before I put on the coffee. It was finally wet again, the porch was soaked, and brittle summer grass had gotten water one more time.

And then, I noticed the mess. There were smelly clothes laid out to air and dry—only they aired and got soggy instead. Shoes were wet, too, since the large, wraparound porch lacked a roof and my children like tossing rather than shelving their shoes.

Before I had even entered this kitchen, I remembered that we had all eaten late, and I hadn't taken time to wipe counters down last night. There would be dirty dishes and a few slivers of grated cheese to greet me this morning. My heart sank a little.

I used to rarely leave dishes at night. I used to have a clean house all the time—but then, I had four messy kids. And because they're happy and healthy, they do things and drop things and leave things.

We had just moved into a four-story house, and each time I scaled a flight of stairs, there was something to pick up on that floor. From the girl's room on the fourth floor to the workout station in the basement, no one in that house loved order as much as I did.

Go figure. I'm the woman who buys color-coordinated nail polish and lines it up on the windowsill. I'm the one who reads interior design books and spends hours gazing at my home to see what I can beautify without spending much money. I'll do things like haul home an old free cabinet set out by the roadside, then spend hours painting, distressing, and waxing it before decorating it carefully.

I'm staring down those soggy gym clothes and it hits me. This house is *supposed to see messes all the time.*

Perhaps, rather than feel that inner growl when I see throw pillows on the floor once again, I should expect them to be there and give my brain that allotted space? Rather than try to keep the schoolroom tidy during school, I should expect that bits of paper will be strewn here and there? Maybe it's OK to have that box of old stuff sit on the bookshelf for my son to grab at a moment's notice, so he can sit and repair in his free time? (Even though I'd much rather see a green houseplant or a nicely framed photo.) Rather than expect the entire house to soothe my nerves, perhaps I should expect it to unravel my nerves.

This house is *supposed to see a mess.* This house is supposed to see many messes, daily.

The inner tension can be replaced with peace when we not only accept what is, but we expect the inevitable and prepare our minds to deal with it.

Peace is possible when I don't allow the mess to spiral out of control for days on end. Children can be required to tidy their rooms and make their beds before they eat breakfast. They can be on dishes duty, daily. The six-year-old can rid the dirty minivan of its various sundry contents while the thirteen-year-old scrubs the bathroom.

We have daily and weekly chores. Cleaning and organizing are scheduled into our lives as much as eating and sleeping.

There's a big difference between constant filth and a daily mess. The former will drive you right into depression while the latter allows for happiness and carefree living.

Mothers, if you're swimming in an unending tide of disaster, perhaps there's a cleaning person you could hire weekly? Or children you could assign those tasks to as soon as they're old enough? Perhaps there's a schedule of chores your kids could accomplish daily. Perhaps there are weekly bathroom duties you could assign yourself or your kids so that you can count on it being done rather than spending two weeks wishing it were done as you step around the scum.

There's a beautiful blend of controlling your environment and letting go of it. We must let go of the daily mess, but not let go of cleaning it up afterward. Tidy homes are a gift to your families, friends, and spouses—places of rest and peace.

Scheduling cleaning has saved me. It's Friday morning and each of my kids knows that today is cleaning day. We will be filling mop buckets and brushing toilet bowls and carrying vacuum cleaners up flights of stairs. All the laundry of the last four days will be cycled through, and there will be this steady beat to the rhythm until things are accomplished for another week.

I'm grateful my mom taught me how to help her. I still remember her asking us to please stop swishing our rags through the air and get busy. I'm grateful she had daily and weekly schedules, and taught me how to do the same just by living her life.

Thank goodness we mothers can accept, expect, and embrace the mess—and then, we get to clean it right up—because accepting an inevitable mess is entirely different than living with endless mess!

Father, thank You for providing rest for our souls when we return to Your good and perfect peace. Help us allow space for everyone in our homes to breathe and enjoy life. Help us to release more peace than pressure into our children's atmosphere.

Day 16

"The Lord is my shepherd; I shall not want. He makes me lie down in green pastures. He leads me beside still waters." (Psalm 23:1&2, ESV)

I stared at the wall hanging in one of my favorite stores, then carefully placed it into my shopping cart.

It was perfect. The words, the font, the message. And I purchased it without guilt because somehow I knew our home "needed" it.

I had just finished cleaning the best gun shop in town while chatting with the bright-eyed little boy who occupied one of the back rooms while his daddy put in a few hours of work. He walked on my wet floor and chattered incessantly when all I wanted was quiet. But he taught me a lesson.

I had left my own little boy at home while I did my weekly job away from the house. It was hard to leave. Somehow, I always feel I'm not being a good mama when I pull out of that driveway by myself. Feeling like not enough is a constant challenge for many of us mothers. But here was a little tyke with eyes so bright and happy they nearly blazed with confidence, and he was, get this, *occupying himself in the back room of a gun shop*. And here I was, feeling bad that my own little boy was running around a large house and property with his babysitter and three siblings.

I wanted to meet the boy's mother. I did get to observe his father, and there was this relaxed, *all is well with our world* type of demeanor. He had the bright face, too.

Mothers, our kids do better with our sometimes-absent bright face than they do with our constantly present, stressed-out countenance.

So often I try to fill every single gap I think I need to fill—and then find myself snappy and exhausted as a result. This summer, I've been taking a step back.

It's hard. I'm wondering if my friends are offended because I haven't had them over as much as I'd like to. I'm wondering if I'm enough, enough, enough—and I'm choosing to let go, anyway.

I fill a gigantic glass jug with granola so the kids can get themselves breakfast before school, and I'm hidden away in my office with my Bible, laptop, and coffee. The next week, I purchase cups of instant cereal at the outlet store for a treat.

I let go of two weekly commitments so I can add in two others that will benefit the whole family. I quit pinching every penny, and I purchase a few lovely things for our home along with teaching DVDs to create a more restful school atmosphere.

We were born to be, not born to perform.

Be kind.

Be loving.

Be full of smiles.

Be rested.

Be connected to the people who matter.

Life is not so much about what we say or do or what model of parenting we choose as it is about what kind of presence we host. The peaceful presence of God determines what we say and do; therefore, taking time to know and commune with God is the most important gift we can give to our children.

Cut your corners but don't cut your time. If you're willing to cut corners you will soon notice that you enjoy your extra time much more than you enjoy the satisfaction of accomplishing everything.

And if you wonder if you're a good enough wife, mother, or friend, remember that *you are a human being more than you are a human doer.*

I'm noticing an extra smile twinge the corners of my mouth these days. I'd rather have extra energy to give out than have no energy because I'm constantly stressed out.

God is a Being, and you are made in His likeness. Because God is the Being He is, He does the things He does. He doesn't do the things He does so He can be the Being He is. In the same way, you can't afford to push too hard to do many things so you can *be something.*

You do the best thing because you already are something—and you don't need to prove what already is.

When you allow His Being to enter your own, you will *be* love, peace, and kindness.

I pick up that wall hanging. I drink that coffee, alone. I have that quiet time. I create space just to be, simply to enjoy, breathe, and smile. I'm done rushing about trying to do everything I think those around me need me to do—because I've seen that doing so much good takes me from *being* all things good.

There is never too much to do—there is only an inner push to be too much because we think we're not enough. Mothers, get this—that push is a lie, and if you need to, drop that paring knife and go purchase onions that are already chopped.

In a burning world, we don't need to be burnt out. We need to be lit right up, because *we were made to be, long before we were stressed with too much to do.*

Father, help us mothers to simply be with You.

DAY 17

You shall teach them diligently to your children, and shall talk of them when you sit in your house, and when you walk by the way, and when you lie down, and when you rise. (Deuteronomy 6:7, ESV)

"You can do it," I encourage the five-year-old.

He's terrified as he feels the wobble of his bike before training wheels hit the ground. Clutching tightly, he begs to be done, but I urge him on as I hold on to his little side to keep him upright. We're on a winding country road close to the bay, where multiple biking groups sail by, often. Today is no exception. These bike speeders whiz past my son with cheers. "You can do it, buddy!"

A child knows little of truth, but will spend his days navigating by his own heart and desires for a path to go down. He will grow into an adult still navigating by his own heart, unless we show him something greater than his own heart to live by.

We may water down truth in search of ease, but fail to see that the richness of truth is precisely what it takes to grab the soul of our child. We must engage his soul to keep his soul. He is unknowingly searching for something greater than himself.

When we promote and live by truth, we lead our children to paths clear enough to walk. We show them light, where once their thoughts were darkened. We lead them up, when their own way would lead them down.

Truth must be pertinent in our own lives if we would have it engage the souls of our children. We can't afford to be mediocre or dull in our walks with Christ. Dull living makes for eager searching, and they may well try to find something more engaging if you haven't shown them the One worth living and dying for.

And you can't say you're willing to die for Christ if you haven't lived for Him fully, with every breath you own, willing to stand for every truth He's shown you.

Your kids know what thrills you. When you're not thrilled with Christ, they may leave for something better. Your own walk is the greatest means Christ will use to draw your child.

It's a bit like the little girl who began sensing God's heart for the church. She went deep with God, because she saw God going deep in her father. She saw his joy; she watched his thrill. She knew God and His ways were the ultimate deciding factor for every single decision in his life, and it drew her in. If Daddy was engaged, excited, and full of purpose, she would find the same joy.

Never water down truth; engage your child in the truth. Show him its beauty and richness.

Truth holds us straight, guides us to good, and changes our course. It can only do so when upheld in its own pristine value. ***When we lower the standard, we confuse our world, but when we keep truth, we clarify our world.***

You will never be satisfied if you walk in unsatisfactory places. Your child will sense this, and will not want to join you. But the opposite is also true. Your child will notice what changes you, thrills you, and draws you in.

Whether or not your child immediately chooses the same, you've shown him something he will always remember.

Love truth and offer to spare your child the pitfalls of his own navigation. Allow him to see a clear path in a murky world; show him a way that keeps him securely in the love of God and path of highest blessing.

And as my little boy was encouraged by random bikers, surround your children with adults who will encourage them. I'm so grateful for people in my world who love my children and provide opportunities for them with the encouragement they need. It truly does take a village to raise a child.

In a world of twirling thought enough to make any head spin, our kids desperately need us and other mentors to be grounded in truth. We are not multiple witnesses in a controversial court case. There is one Witness testifying truth from every angle, in all things.

We get to hear the judge speak clearly, and because our God is not a human judge, He is always right. Voices of belief may clamor for our attention just as multiple, conflicting voices seek to drown out each other in a courtroom. Because our judge is always right, we get to be right when we follow Him; right on the path to surest blessing and clearest vision. Steering our kids along in this way is the greatest gift we can give them, because truth is born out of love for our highest blessing and greatest good.

Our children's legs may be wobbly as they learn to balance that bike, and their hearts may be unsteady until they grab hold of truth in the lovely person of Jesus Christ. Let's hold steady until they grab hold of a steady God.

Lord Jesus, help us honor You by honoring Your Word. You are steadfast, never changing, immovable, and good. Your truth is part of Your love.

DAY 18

Do not rebuke an older man but encourage him as you would a father.
(1 Timothy 5:1, ESV)

The young teenage girl spoke vehemently, and I watched the older lady—her mother—wilt. We were both navigating the same respect problem with a few of our teens, and were in this together, trying to come up with solutions.

I watched the mother wilt because she knew what I saw—that tones of such a nature are rarely becoming when directed toward a person three times your senior. It was awkward. But more than that, sad. How honor loses its seat in our society baffles me. Yet as the girl spoke, I knew there was truth in what she was saying—but her mother would not be able to hear it because it was spoken with such disrespect.

Years of the same old had brought the ugly side forth. Like a dam waiting to burst, the girl's heart had finally had enough, and she was letting her mother know. But in letting her mother know, there was an even more vital thing she didn't know.

Honesty can be spoken with honor.

There is little left in our culture to properly define and exemplify true honor. In other cultures, we read of children standing when a parent enters the room; here, parents are sassed and disrespected while kids slouch in front of the TV, remote in hand, guiding their way through another movie which most likely feeds even more disrespect.

What are we feeding our kids? And why?

It's not uncommon to walk into a home and have a child ignore your presence completely because his eyes are glued to his video game. If you say hello, you get a quick, reluctant response as if you're not worth the time and effort to greet.

In our culture it is not unusual to see men wilt while wives emasculate them and strip them of their dignity—in public, at that. We forget that to a man, honor speaks love—just as to a woman, time, tenderness, and affection speak love.

We attribute a man's need for honor to an egotistic desire for recognition and status while forgetting that they were created a certain way for a reason—*and it's not sexist to affirm that need and put forth effort to meet it.*

In many other cultures, the elderly are cared for, respected, and seated at the table with their families; in our culture, they are often passed over, neglected as grown kids run their own families, and despised as "old fashioned" when they try to speak wisdom into a younger generation.

In 1 Samuel, when David was on the run trying to escape a wicked king who was hunting him down out of sheer jealousy, he had opportunity to kill the king himself. Rather, he cut a corner off Saul's robe as he slept—and later berated himself for doing so. He warned his men not to kill God's anointed.

His honor moved Saul to repentance and he returned from his jealousy-driven manhunt in shame (1 Samuel 24).

David was able to show honor because he first possessed it. Only when honor is known vertically (with God) can we show it horizontally (to others).

The young girl mentioned previously was obviously frustrated with her relationship with her mother.

"You need to be honest with your mother, but you must change your tone. There's a way to own your feelings without degrading her," I told her.

We can twist our faces into an angry knot—or we can express our feelings in a loving manner.

We can speak vehemently and forcefully—or we can allow truth spoken in love to work its own force.

"Your mother needs to hear the truth," I urged the young lady. "But she will hear hard things spoken in a soft way much better than she will wade through a rebellious attitude. Allow raw truth spoken in love to work its own power."

When we learn to speak honorably, we have an open door to speak even more clearly. *Honor never implies shutting down or putting up with wrong or hurtful things.*

We often mistake pretense for honor, but nothing could be further from the truth.

Being an honorable person simply means that you show respect as you disagree with another. Others will listen more carefully to you—not less—when you begin to know and possess your own honor.

Honoring others is not only for their benefit, but also for yours. When you see the value God places on you, you will hesitate to represent yourself in a manner others find distasteful and hurtful. No one, not even your girlfriends, appreciates seeing a woman put down.

Mothers can show a younger generation how to be honest with honor when they know how to speak out difficult things in a spirit of love. The young girl didn't need to be quiet—she just needed to speak the truth in love (Ephesians 4:15).

Lord Jesus, helps us show our children by example what it means to be honest with honor. Help us not wilt under mistreatment but use our voices honorably to express what we need. Help us teach our children the same thing. Set us free to express our hearts while showing Your love at the same time.

DAY 19

In your hearts honor Christ the Lord as holy, always being prepared to make a defense to anyone who asks you for a reason for the hope that is in you. (1 Peter 3:15, ESV)

The day I was cleaning for the neighbor, head bent low over the tub while a heated ceiling light blazed down on my back, was also the day I tucked my phone in my pocket and turned on my favorite app.

Podcasts keep me learning and engaged during the most menial tasks. And as I cleaned, I noticed around me books regarding Buddhism and meditation while the speaker resounded truth in my ear.

Everyone's looking for happiness and peace. We don't always find it in the ways we think we will, and the human soul is on a constant quest for the ever-elusive joy to permeate our days.

Everyone wonders what to do with the pain in this world.

One of the most important aspects of mothering is to teach our children how to handle the problem of pain. The invasive difficulties of life are one of the surest causes to lead a person away from Christ.

How can a good God allow pain and tragedy? Talking with our kids about the dilemma long before they reach adulthood is mothering at the core of its beauty. We are not here just to feed them dinner and read them stories. We are here to prepare their hearts to absorb Christ for all eternity.

It's so easy for us to lack vision. We become nearsighted, focusing so intently on basic needs which keep us running like some hamster on a wheel. For heaven's sake, when will we speak to them of heavenly things? When will we bring eternity into their hearts by preparing them with tools needed to keep their hearts?

It's also easy to become fearful, choosing to ignore questions we feel ill equipped to answer—or perhaps have never found answers for, ourselves. This is one of the reasons I turn on that app as I scrub tubs and toilets. I want to be prepared to give an answer not only to others, but first of all to my kids. (1 Peter 3:15)

Ignoring the weightier matters of our faith while tending to lesser things means ruin for the souls of our children. Sooner or later our kids will encounter people or situations that make them question deep matters of life, God, and morality. Make sure they already have a foundation to address those questions based on what they've learned from you and their own walks with God.

A few weeks ago I sat in a homeschool co-op class and was thrilled to see them teaching their students about worldviews in opposition to Christianity. The teacher delved into new spirituality, Islam, and Marxism without hesitation. Students were taught the basics of each religion and ideology along with the problems with each.

My own daughter is currently reading *Darwin's Demise*, which explains what Darwin believed, why he believed it, and the arguments against his beliefs.

I don't recommend a premature diet of alternative religions. Deception can overtake the mind of a child or teen quickly. I'm advocating for an open, honest relationship with your child where you as the parent and chief spiritual leader guide them through some of the toughest and most basic fundamental questions of the faith.

I'm advocating that we broach these questions with solid answers long before the world brings them to their attention.

I try to teach my children personally, but another thing I do is utilize a Sunday-evening apologetics class taught by a man in my church. Twice a month, on a Sunday evening, I pack up the car and bring the children to a living room environment where they can relax, have snacks, and hear quality teaching on logic, critical thinking, and the basis for our faith.

Children will have questions whether or not we are comfortable with them. Will we allow them to try to answer them on their own, or will we lead them slowly and certainly to be able to defend their faith while they are still with us?

I listened to Ken Ham's DVD series "The Foundations," when the kids were young. I addressed the problem of pain in my own living room where the kids openly asked questions regarding my faith. I am not threatened by these questions, even when there are times I wished I knew how to answer more sufficiently.

I sat with the dear old lady I cleaned for and listened as she spoke of her beliefs. She didn't know what would happen to her after death—most of her security seemed to be based on her ability to think positively.

The stark realization is that death comes to all of us whether or not we think positively. We need more than our own thoughts to depend on.

Thank God we have more to offer our kids—but we must feed them words of life before the world feeds them thoughts of death. Utilize wonderful apologists and creationists when you need to learn more of these things.

Father, thank You that even though there are mysteries we won't understand until heaven, You've shown us more than enough reasons to believe. Help us know those truths ourselves so we can share them with our children.

DAY 20

Jesus wept. (John 11:35, ESV)

"Mom, why is God so mean to good people?" one of my children asked during Bible time. "You've done little wrong your entire life and still, you've gone through such hardships."

My eyes popped a little. First of all, I've done plenty wrong because I have needs, sins, and faults like everyone. Second, God is the greatest Source of love I've known and I don't think of Him as being mean to me.

Gently, I try to explain why I still choose to trust God in spite of my pain.

Learning about God for ourselves is the most powerful mothering tool we have.

John chapter 11 tells of Lazarus's sickness, and Jesus choosing to stay away even though he knew how deadly it was. Jesus didn't go to Lazarus's home until he knew Lazarus was dead, and even then, he waited four days.

He didn't love Lazarus or His sisters any less by being absent, but He was up to something greater than avoiding human sorrow. Some things are best birthed through sorrow than any other avenue. Look at Jesus's love as He showed up.

Martha tells Jesus that if he had been there, her brother would still be alive. Jesus becomes deeply moved and begins to weep, telling them that *if they would believe, they would see the glory of God.*

He wanted them to believe before He raised Lazarus from the dead. He wanted them to believe in the midst of their tears and darkest hour. He wasn't there to heal Lazarus immediately, but wanted them to see Him weep, then see His power.

Jesus enters our pain, and there, we find Him more than before. Our children need to know that a perfect world will only come in eternity, that sin brought pain to this world, and that, in the end, Christ will overcome all sin, pain, and death.

Jesus never caused sin, which is the blame for all pain in this world. But He's here to redeem this earth in the middle of its story ridden with pain as a result of human choices.

Mary and Martha were part of a greater story than their own small world. Jesus healed Lazarus so that others would see the glory of the God-miraculous.

In the same manner, He resurrects us in our troubles and pain. There's light to be seen, and it is seen even better in darkness. *Light always shines brighter in darkness.*

When God gives grace to suffering martyrs, when they sing at the stake, when they bravely allow themselves to be thrown into icy waters with their hands tied, all without denying Christ—do you not think that the grace of Jesus Christ and the glories of heaven become breathtakingly real?

See this—in each trial, there is a kingdom solution that rises with power and glory. Resurrection power can be seen, known, and experienced long before Jesus returns because He's given us His Presence in the form of a Comforter.

Teach your kids, parents. Give them no excuse to say, "There's more peace over here with Buddha than there is at home with God."

This will take spirit-filled living. You simply must display the glories of Christ to your kids or they will want nothing to do with your Jesus. If you live in constant discord and tension while you express belief in a peace-giving, loving God, they will wonder at the disconnect between your words and your experience. When you do mess up and create an ugly atmosphere, simply ask their forgiveness and they will see that God came for Mama, too—because Mama is human and she also needs Jesus. Your apology will be more of a powerful influence to them than your perfection would be.

God cannot be God unless what He stands for is absolute. This we know both by experience and written word, that God is the Father of comfort and Founder of love.

"God is anything but mean," I smile at my child. "In fact, He comes to take away the effects of evil in this world and take us to be with him forever when we die. He cannot be tempted with evil and He only undoes what the enemy tries to accomplish. Love wins!"

Jesus, thank You that You weep with us mothers in all the things that bring us sorrow. Thank You that You meet us there and show us how good You are. Thank you for leaving the Comforter with us when You ascended to heaven.

DAY 21

Thou therefore endure hardness as a good soldier of Jesus Christ.
(2 Timothy 2:3, ESV)

I stared at the emptier house. Strange how one child can make such a difference.

She had flown home with my mother to help her auntie for three weeks. Excitement was high, and as could be expected, she didn't miss us very much at all because she was surrounded with aunties and uncles and cousins and grandparents.

I sobered up when I realized my little girl who had grown taller than her mother was out and away—*and loving it.*

And when it was time for her to come home, she picked up the phone and asked if I could change her ticket to allow her to stay another month.

It stung just a little.

I had a choice—rejoice in the good roots she was establishing with my awesome family, or be hurt that she didn't miss her mama. And I realized once again that hard doesn't always mean bad.

Sometimes the best things in life can only be accomplished through the hard things. We naturally try to avoid the hard—but what if we embraced it, instead? What if, when something felt difficult, we dug right in and saw the end we were trying to achieve?

Mothering is hard. Toddler years get replaced with teen years—and all of them are so full of need that your own needs get tossed aside.

But mothering is the best thing that ever happened to me. The love I get to carry, the hands I get to hold, the hearts I get to nurture are such blessings to my own life that I often forget the hard in light of the joy.

When the newborn squeaked in wee hours of the night, I'd groan momentarily, then be overcome with sheer love and delight at being able to care for the squeaky little bundle depending on me.

When the same child grows tall, independent, and adventurous, I groan a bit—then get overcome with joy at the blessings she's experiencing in her own life. It costs me a little, but all good things cost something.

My own redemption cost a lot. God gave His own Son to carry my sin, when He had never sinned. Really?

It was hard enough that even the Son of God had great drops of sweat running right down to the ground. But He knew the hard of the night meant the good of the entire world.

Mothers, let's cease avoiding the hard. Let's walk right through hard places bravely because we see the goodness of the end goal. Sometimes this means engaging grief for a while so we can process it and come through the other side. Never deny your feelings; rather, engage them so you can find what God is saying to you through them.

Be OK with grief. Sit with it, and don't avoid it. Through it, God will equip you with whatever you need to come to the other side with Him. This is true for smaller things like children leaving the house, or for larger things like death or betrayal. We can only come through something healthily if we take time to engage it truthfully. Negative emotions can be used to make us seek out solid answers for the lack in our lives.

God wastes nothing.

Life is triumphant when we see the end goal. A mother in labor may groan for hours, but be willing to endure for the joy of her child's life. In the same way, each season of life brings something to groan about—but even more to rejoice over.

I'd rather choose the rejoicing part! If your babies are small, load them up and go have fun, anyway. If they are teens, choose the best for them even if your heart creaks a little.

My daughter's home again, but I know that very soon she will leave for good. And I'm making the most of the remaining years with her so that I can smile when she's walking away, right into the rest of her life.

Hard can mean *good.* Hard can even mean best.

Lord Jesus, give us strength to make way for good things by enduring hard things.

Day 22

And you will know the truth, and the truth will make you free. (John 8:32, ESV)

I had asked the question a million times, "What is forgiveness?" Then, I'd asked another question, "Is it OK to be angry?"

My circumstances forced me out of the usual "don't ever be angry" stance I tried to live by. Suddenly, life was so raw that I took a good look at Jesus's feelings when He tipped over money tables and ordered the vendors out of His temple (Matthew 21:12–13).

I pondered the fact that Jesus called mercy and truth to meet up, and righteousness and peace to unite. He wasn't asking for mercy and peace only, but wanted it to unite with equal doses of righteousness and truth.

In fact, seeing God's mercy as it really is allows for nothing else. God is not only mercy; He is also truth. In fact, truth is merciful and mercy is truthful. In Christ, they cannot be separated.

God's incredible mercy doesn't blithely pass over murder, rape, abuse, or any other wrong we see in this world. And in all honesty, those who say "don't judge" the most are often those who ask for judgment most *when an offense happens to them.*

God's love doesn't accept all things; it changes all things.

"Love and acceptance" never meant accepting harmful behavior. God's love calls for His judgment of those things, or He wouldn't be love at all.

The mantra "don't judge, and accept everyone" is very quickly used by guilty parties to project their own guilt onto those who dare speak up against wrong. This is such a far cry from what Jesus meant when He asked us not to judge each other that there is no comparison between the two.

Divine love cannot "accept and not judge" things that hurt and harm the people He loved and died for. Love can only accept things that line up to the heart of God.

God is love and He gets to interpret the meaning of it.

Time passed by as I kept asking God to show me what it truly meant to forgive. I'll never forget the day I was driving in my car while my little boy asked a million questions about life and God, when it suddenly all came together in my heart.

Forgiveness meant seeing God's heart for the offender. It meant hiding nothing, but speaking the truth on all accounts. Then, it meant releasing the offender into the hands of God and those in charge while I walked free, having given it over after doing my part.

I'd met plenty of women who interpreted forgiveness as denial. After many years of pushing things to some back corner of their mind, they were still crying and trying to "forgive." I'd also met women who couldn't stop talking about what happened to them and seemed bent on bringing justice while the offense was strewn around constantly.

I wanted neither. How could mercy and truth meet up like Jesus talked about?

My situation compelled me to say yes when two sets of detectives asked to talk. Honesty led me to speak the truth of all I knew.

Sisters, the truth sets us free. The truth of everything, all the time, in all situations leads us to God's solution for everything, all the time, in all circumstances.

Embracing the truth of hard things allows us to move from the hard into better things.

How can you find internal release from something you haven't owned up to or dealt with? Denial cages your soul while truth brings you to freedom. Trust me, I know.

God's remedy for women is never silent suffering. It is always truth, help, and solutions.

My soul found an incredible release from my situation as I placed the outcome of all things into the hand of a God who cared for me and my children more than I can comprehend. I watched Him move— and hear me carefully on this—because I had done my part, I was able to let it go in complete trust.

When our souls find absolute rest in the outcome of our circumstances, we know forgiveness has found its place.

Forgiveness is not denial; it is rest.

Forgiveness doesn't accept all things; it leads us to release all things.

Forgiveness doesn't mean shutting up when you need to speak up; it does mean speaking with grace and truth regardless of your circumstance.

All of us have something in our lives to forgive. A proper understanding of what forgiveness truly is, is one of the best gifts we can give our children.

In short, forgiveness is internally breaking free from your situation after you've walked through it, honestly dealt with it, then put it behind you and moved on to better things.

Rather than become bitter, you become better.

You can think of the circumstance without being taken over by it. You can release both the offender and the offense, having them not only out of your life, but out of your heart.

Whatever you don't let go of still holds you captive. But, whatever thing someone meant to hurt you with is undone when you release it and learn from it, instead. As Corrie Ten Boom says, **"There is no pit so deep where God's love isn't deeper.**

Forgiveness is a gift to yourself. It's also one of the most important lessons you can teach your children. Let them see you free in spirit from whatever meant to crush you. Fly free!

Father, thank You that You care for us so deeply that You never blindly accept harmful things done against us. Thank You that You are in charge and we can trust You completely as we follow Your heart for us. Thank You for bringing us sweet release from hurtful things and leading us into deeper understanding of Your love and freedom.

DAY 23

It is in vain that you rise up early and go late to rest, eating the bread of anxious toil; for he gives to his beloved sleep. (Psalm 127:2, ESV)

Messy house.
Messy hair.
Messy kids.
Messy bed.

Today was going to be different.

Yesterday I felt a bit like one of those spinning, buzzing bees that had been mortally wounded but still lived. Hot flashes coursed through my entire body and my head spun so thickly I could barely think.

I pushed, even though I knew I was sick and my body needed to stop. Like, *really stop*.

No good mother goes back to bed when the kids are waiting to learn math and language and science and five other things, I thought.

By the end of the day, I was yelling at the kids. Well, my version of yelling is raising my voice just a little, and being upset about things that should be handled calmly. But after dinner, as we all relaxed under my reading of *Robin Hood*, I promised the kids that tomorrow Mama wouldn't yell, and we would do things differently.

Today I stayed in my pajamas until afternoon. The kids got their own meals. We did school in my bed.

None of the four cared that I had messy hair and was wearing flannel pj's. The oldest son crawled into bed and gave me a laughing fit until my stomach hurt. The oldest daughter wrote an entire page of hospital instructions for me to follow. The little ones were happy to be little.

My body was weak, but my heart was happy and my thoughts regained positive momentum.

Mothers, our little ones feel the tension we create. They would much rather us feel good than look perfect. They would much rather us have a happy face than the house be spotless. They would much rather have less for Christmas than have us stressed about one more thing.

I remember the Mother's Day when, before the day was over, I dissolved in tears with exhaustion over it all.

Why? All day I had been hearing how great, wonderful, caring, and important mothers are. I knew it was all true and I loved being a mama to four kids whom I was genuinely proud of. I stood with the other mothers at church and received roses like all the rest. But I was tired. So tired.

All day Saturday I had them out in the sunshine enjoying a parade and logging show. Their safety and well-being rested on my shoulders. I loved spending the day with them, but . . .

It was their fighting. Ugh! The girls weren't getting along, and their constant arguing was making me miserable.

By Sunday, in spite of dressing up and receiving flowers and chocolate, I was so drained I felt sick. Exhausted. What was I doing wrong?

I decided to rest and quit trying to do more things to make the day perfect. Rather, I went to bed.

And then it was Monday morning. Guess what? I was tired, yes, but I was alive again and loving my life. Breakfast got made, a pot of coffee brewed, and bowls of oatmeal were served to the kids. We sang and prayed together, and I took a meal to a sick friend. I worked out and drank protein. The schoolbooks came out, and little heads bent low over books.

Public school was coming in later years, but at that season, it was home school. During both seasons, I had to work hard at rest because my natural impulse is to push. Learning to slow down has been the greatest gift I've given myself—and some of it happened because other well-meaning people repeatedly encouraged me to rest. I am forever grateful to them.

Life is beautiful.

Allow yourself to cry, to stop, to be done. You will get up again, and you will do well.

Because nothing worth fighting for comes easy, and mothers hold the future in their hands.

Father, thank You that as we offer rest to our children,
You offer rest to us. Thank You for taking care of us, Your daughters.
Help us receive the care You offer.

DAY 24

Do not lay up for yourselves treasures on earth, where moth and rust
destroy and where thieves break in and steal, but lay up for yourselves
treasures in heaven, where neither moth nor rust destroys and where
thieves do not break in and steal. For where your treasure is, there your
heart will be also. (Matthew 6:19–21, ESV)

I rocked him, this youngest son who was too big to be all wrapped up
in a pink blanket. But I did it anyway.

Summer is nearing an end, and the minivan has been filled to the
brim with kids, sand, frogs, and snakes. My twelve-year-old daughter,
who is old enough to realize she wants to look good, sees us in another
car's window reflection one day.

"Mama." Her tone is sober. "I just saw our reflection and we *look*
terrible in this minivan."

The thought of being Mama in one of those dusty vans I once
vowed never to own strikes a chord way deep, and I laugh until the
tears come. Yes, it is always dirty, and even dented. But kids and lake
days and ice cream-filled summer days make it all worth it. And *though*
I'd love to look good, I love even more to live well.

I pray peace over the sleeping child with the blue cast on his arm,
and heaven touches us at the close of day.

The hutch is full of new books, and as summer days close, school days begin. I face it with excitement and trepidation, because I know my weakness when four kids need me at once, when there are papers and books scattered everywhere, and my brain has no repose because there's demand on full charge with not enough supply.

Or so it seems. *In reality, doesn't a good God supply enough moments in a day?* Perhaps we just create too much to accomplish with the time He gives.

I carry the sleeping child to his bed and smother him in a thousand kisses. He melts me. He breaks me. How could I ever be worthy of caring for one, let alone four, of God's little people?

Lord, help me create peace more than pressure, rest more than rush, a haven more than an atmosphere of haste.

Because it's in the quiet moments when we get to share the deeper things of life with our kids. In peaceful nights we get to open that Bible and talk long with them about all that really matters.

And what matters isn't looking good with a nice car or the right fashion statement. The greatest statement we can give our kids is that we are unconcerned with the world because we are taken with Christ.

I drive this minivan on purpose so I can work less and *mother with purpose.*

Let fashion judge me as I drive around in a dusty van loaded with kids and look *terrible*—but let not my kids grow up without being taught about God and all things near to His heart.

Father, help us pave the way to eternity each day by making way for things of eternal value here on earth. Help our statements be of You more than of this world.

Day 25

Honor your father and your mother, that your days may be long in the land that the Lord your God is giving you. (Exodus 20:12, ESV)

I saw the look of consternation on the mother's face as her teen faced her off with rapidly engaging opinions conflicting her own.

The mother was tender—and her child was tough.

The mother didn't create conflict and never engaged conflict voluntarily. She's one of the most giving people I know and we all want to be around her because there's one word to describe her: *comfort.*

Then, God handed her a child who would let her know that she couldn't always be sweet.

She had to say "No." She had to stay in conversations where the heat was burning too close for comfort. She had to learn how to be strong enough in her own person that her identity didn't come from her child being pleased.

People-pleasing mothers fall hard on their faces when they can no longer please their children on all accounts. It's easy for them to get up at night with sick children, easy to give their heart and soul for constant needs—but let me tell you this, learning to stand strong is as uncomfortable as walking on ice with bare feet.

Stacey was a strong-natured child who is now a mature, happily married wife and mother. She shared with me one day that as a teen, she fought her mother on most things in life and her mother would often give in.

Stacey shares today that her respect level went down each time her mother gave in. Though I'm sure her mother was trying to show love or trying "not to be difficult," Stacey rather interpreted it as weakness.

Strong children want to be met with strength. They may buck hard but they crave a wall to buck into.

Contrary to our natural thoughts, children crave boundaries. They need rules. And they desperately need to be held accountable to these boundaries. Knowing they are not in charge brings a sense of peace because they no longer bear too much responsibility.

When we allow our child to make his own decisions, we unknowingly place a burden too great for him to bear. He becomes crankier and more rebellious as a result.

Enforcing parental guidance with kindness and firmness brings a whole new world of security for your child. He knows where he belongs. And so do you.

Mothers, next time you want to cave in to a strong child or be offended by some conversation you've had to be in, remember this—all strong children need a strong wall to buck into that won't budge when they need safety and boundaries.

Father, help us to not take disrespect personally. Help us guide our children to honest communication spoken honorably. Help us not to shut them down but teach them how to express their feelings without hurtful attitudes. Help us be humble enough to welcome their input in our lives.

Day 26

By working hard in this way we must help the weak and remember the words of the Lord Jesus, how he himself said, "It is more blessed to give than to receive." (Acts 20:35, ESV)

It was Monday morning.

You know, those Mondays where the laundry is overflowing and everyone is exhausted from a busy weekend. It was a leftover oatmeal and green juice kind of a morning, with schoolwork to do and, well, you get the picture!

To top it off, my three-year-old son decided to be *all boy* that morning. By 9:30, he managed to pull the cat's legs, kick the dog, pee on the floor when he was trying to get it into the toilet, poop into the toilet and boast about how large his deposit was, catch a spider and carry it into the house as it was writhing in distress, allow the cat to run inside twice, bring stink bugs into the house and beg to let them swim in the toilet, dump a bucket of bleached T-shirts onto the porch floor and spill his prized container of airsoft BBs over them, bug his siblings numerous times, beg for a Tupperware to house his "dinky bug," eat two servings of breakfast, and need his second pair of jeans.

And it wasn't just the little tot.

That day my life just didn't feel great. I was tired of feeding people, folding laundry, and teaching math. Tired of wiping messy counters when I would rather put on my running shoes and feel fresh air in my lungs.

Today, anything but this! But responsibility doesn't run away, and deep inside I knew this was a phase and my joy in mothering would return. It took courage that day, and a whole lot of patience.

It does every day. It is so easy to lose vision.

I write about my emotionally challenged day to encourage you. If you feel this way, you are not alone. Being a mama takes patience, and perhaps even more, it takes courage. Courage to believe that what you're doing is important enough to give yourself to, to use your energy up with, and to focus on.

Courage to smile, dance, and delight in the sunshine of the day even when it's been a stormy one.

Courage to love and give when you want to quit.

Mothers, may I encourage you that you are of the bravest, most courageous? The hands that rock the cradle, clean pee off the floor, read the Bible before bedtime, and buy another gallon of milk are the hands that rule the nation.

We may forget this in difficult moments, but it comes alive during times like the following moment I had with our little boy.

Ready for bed, his little voice lisps, "Mama's bed?" I can't deny him, so he crawls in. Next, "Mama, cuddle me? Uh, cozy." My heart melts into a puddle.

I crawl in and he snuggles up, cheeks warm from his day in the sunshine, eyes drooping. Our arms are locked. I am fit to burst.

To be a mother is to experience some of the grandest love the world has ever known. It is no wonder that God says, "Can a woman forget her nursing child, and not have compassion on the son of her womb? Surely they may forget, yet I will not forget you" (Isaiah 49:15 NKJV).

Being a mother allows me to taste in a small way the great love God has for us. Even a mother may forget, a mother with all the natural, God-given instincts to nurture and love.

But God never will. And in all moments, whether good or bad, you won't either.

Like when you're brushing your teeth and one son comes into the bathroom for a hug while another waits at the door with his math book.

At the same time you notice how dirty the sink is, and fleetingly wonder whether you should take time to clean it, or just walk away.

You turn around to see the bathtub is disgusting so you deal with it halfway, pull the shower curtain shut, and hope the next person in won't be upset.

You pull waffles out of the freezer for breakfast while berating yourself for not having something healthier prepared.

You help one child with school while the other two are talking in your ear.

Your son (he wouldn't want you to know how old he is) asks for a hug and says he hasn't gotten any yet today. You remind him that you did give him one while brushing your teeth. He says, "Oh, I thought you told me I was being annoying and told me to go away."

You burst into a laugh and start the hugging process all over again. He lives up the moment and in no time is standing on the table pretending to be someone tall enough to reach down to Mama. Who knows whether I really did hug him earlier or not—by now my brain is a bit foggy.

At recess time the oldest daughter wants a walk and expresses that she needs time alone but it's hard to come by. I agree. Time alone in a family is delicious, especially when quality time means more to you than most people. So one daughter gets a walk and by evening the other daughter stands at the door asking for time to chat. You're so exhausted that you tell her she needs to wait for tomorrow.

Tomorrow comes, and there is new energy.

Did you know that even though parents get less sleep, less time doing hobbies, fewer date nights, and basically less of everything, surveys reveal they are more joyful?

Keep giving, and you'll join those who wonder where the joy came from!

Father, You are the Ultimate Giver. Thank You that following You means giving of ourselves in ways that count. Give us vision and insight into what that looks like, and grant us Your joy as we do so.

Day 27

And let us consider how to stir up one another to love and good works, not neglecting to meet together, as is the habit of some, but encouraging one another, and all the more as you see the Day drawing near. (Hebrews 10: 24–25, ESV)

Many parents pride themselves in teaching first-time obedience and not allowing their children to question their authority. Without listening and drawing out the thoughts of the child, they establish rules and boundaries to be obeyed immediately and without question. A child who questions or has a conflicting opinion is considered out of order and less than obedient. As a result, these kids often grow up with a subdued, apathetic spirit. *They are there, but nobody's home.*

These kids often grow up without the ability to speak publicly or share their gifts with the world in confidence. Their true, vibrant selves are dulled. They often have difficulty making decisions or feeling sure about anything. They've been taught to shut down their own thoughts for the sake of compliance and unquestioning obedience.

Of course, young children must be taught to obey. But as they grow older, they must be allowed to share their thoughts and voice questions. This can all be done in a respectful manner, after which he or she still yields to the parent if there remains a conflict of opinion.

Parents of growing kids often mistake voiceless compliance for obedience.

Allow your child to question your decision. You want him to grow into a thinking, reasoning, confident adult, after all. When he voices his thoughts, answer him respectfully and honestly. If he is right on something you're missing, freely acknowledge it and give him credit for his wisdom.

Purpose to move on in the best way more than your own way.

My relationship with my daughter suffered until I learned how important justice was to her. I learned not to simply shut her down when she showed attitude. I needed to acknowledge anything she was saying that was true, then move on to bring her to a place of respect and obedience. Once I was able to let go of my own fear of being hurt or humiliated, I was able to say, "Yes, you're right and you have a great idea," even when I had just voiced something entirely different.

Sometimes our kids are more right than we are. Digging in our heels when we know they have a good thought shows an incredible lack of humility and inner wholeness as a mother.

Our emotions gain control when we use the power of our parenthood, rather than the power of goodness and truth.

Kids obey better when they see that you are also under authority, when they see you governed by truth—even if that truth is coming from their lips. They see you overcome your pride and bend to truth even when it costs you, even when you want to dig in your heels just to be "right."

By bending to truth, you will gain respect rather than lose more of it.

When you willingly defer to all truth, you have an honest platform from which to ask for respect and obedience. Your child will so admire your own heart given to truth and goodness that he will also be quicker to humble himself when needed.

As our kids grow, we must earn their respect more than demand it. We must relate, converse, speak, and reason with our child. We must honor them.

When their wishes are neither right nor wrong, sometimes they need to know we won't comply to their wishes when their attitudes are out of line. *This will help them master their attitudes while still expressing their thoughts.*

Or, we can change course due to the truth or goodness they've seen even though it's been given in a disrespectful manner. Then, we can move on to discuss the disrespect and deal with it if needed.

The key is to listen and acknowledge their thoughts and feelings. Whether you change course or not may be entirely up to you as you determine what will help your child most.

We cannot afford to disregard their wishes each time, neither can we always change course. Seasons and circumstances change, which means mothers need to keep an open heart during conversations so they can discern what each child needs in a given scenario.

As I jokingly used to tell my small children when they didn't want to listen to each other, "Always listen to anything that's true or right, even if it comes from a mouse's mouth."

They'd laugh, and get the point. They could listen to and receive truth even if it came from a younger sibling. Mothers, we can do the same!

Lord Jesus, help us to encourage our children by creating fellowship with our children.

DAY 28

Jesus answered, "We must work the works of Him who sent me while it is day; night is coming, when no one can work." (John 9:3a &4, ESV)

Prioritizing and managing time is a complex topic for busy moms. My own mother made it seem effortless, but looking back I realize how very disciplined and giving she was to create a home like she did.

Beyond menial tasks, there are things calling our name, things we want to make time for. When we understand how to manage our time well, we sometimes (not always) end up with pockets of time for the things we love.

What you are good at is often a great indicator of what you should prioritize. I have friends who can paint the world on a canvas, others who can make people feel exceptionally loved, others who can turn out tasty dishes and drinks as if they had years of culinary school. And we all know there are busy moms who travel the world doing business some of us know nothing of.

God equips His daughters for His deeds in His world. Trying to copy another is an extravagant waste of time and robs the world of the one life only you can live.

Live as best as you can, and you won't miss your purpose. Draw near to the heart of God and give out what He breathes in. Live all of it with delight—and if you feel there's no delight to be had, know there is still joy to be known—because you are a free agent and you get to choose the posture of your heart!

Part of choosing the posture of our hearts is choosing to manage time wisely. This can greatly increase the peace in our homes and lives! Following are some tips I learned along the way, some as a child from watching my mother.

1. *Keep your cooking simple.*
You might cringe in my kitchen if you're a foodie!

It's not rare for me to make a crockpot of plain beans and serve them more than once. Costco carries raw-but-rolled-out flour tortillas, and I purchase large containers of cheese, sour cream, and salsa. If we're lucky we get guacamole (good grief, why are avocados so exorbitantly priced?). Or, I'll do a huge pot of stir-fried veggies and chicken, and again it lasts for more than one day.

If I cook a simple dinner and don't mind leftovers, I might get time for a nap, reading, or gardening. Truth be told, I'd rather have a clean house than a fancy dinner. Some of you may be the opposite, and you could put my table to shame with your lovely dinners each night! It's OK to be different and to prioritize different things in your home as long as your family's needs are met.

2. *Keep paper towels and wipes on hand everywhere.*
Seriously, this is no joke!

I used to try to save money by not using them all the time, but those days have long gone. Frugality is not always a virtue. Keeping paper towels and wipes under the bathroom sink ensures a quick wipe down of the sink and toilet when it's needed. Keeping wipes in the car gives you peace of mind when you discover a child with breakfast still on his face just as you lift him out of the car seat before church.

3. *Buy bottled water for the car.*

If you're a busy mom with little ones, filling those water bottles (where are the lids, anyway?) is the last thing you need to stress about as you're rushing out the door. Pay a few extra dollars and buy water for the car as you purchase milk for the fridge.

4. *Decrease your kids' activities.*

This one is huge. Peace in the home disintegrates greatly if mom's minivan is constantly on the run. Some moms give their child one away-from-home option—if they do sports, they don't do music, and vice versa. When you are constantly running kids everywhere, you lose out on priceless moments of baking together, teaching them how to clean, or be available to help others. Nowadays, kids are raised to perform more than to serve—but that is an entire subject in itself, and one that merits more attention than can be given here.

5. *Shop secondhand clothes, and take all your older children with you for a day.*

Making one shopping day for all of them not only saves time and gas, it gives you all a day together. I love loading mine in the car and helping them choose clothes for the next school year. We eat out, or if finances are scarce, we run into a grocery store, pull treats off the shelf, and eat in the car. We have fun because we make it fun. The girls pull name-brand clothing from thrift store racks for a fraction of the usual price—and we all go home happy.

6. *Assign chores to your children.*

Each day brings opportunity to teach your child contribution.

Make lists of what needs to be done, tailor cut for each child—some daily lists, some weekly. Mothers, you don't need to do everything! My older children clean my bathrooms and scour my kitchen while I pay bills and put groceries away. My youngest has a daily list of chores, things I pull out of thin air for him to accomplish because he needs it and so do I. Children need to feel vital to our homes and we do them a favor by requiring them to help out.

7. Pack lunches the night before.
This one saved me. Who wants to spread mayonnaise at 6:00 a.m.? While the kids do dinner dishes, I can pack lunches for the next day. Not only that, I can have quick and easy breakfasts available for each child to grab. Sometimes I'll make quiche or eggs ahead of time and it lasts a few days for those of us who need protein. No one has to cook in the morning rush before school. You can even use a Keurig machine for coffee! (And don't be afraid of real cream—every mother deserves heavy cream in her coffee each day!)

8. Do laundry twice a week.
Having scheduled laundry days allows you to know which day to throw in a load before heading out the door. Finishing the same day is important, and younger children can help with this, especially carrying it to the proper rooms. Getting laundry done saves a mountain of hassle as no one is yelling for socks they don't have or underwear they can't find. Older kids can do their own laundry, leaving you with less to take care of.

9. Deep clean once a week.
Tidying up can and should be done daily, but deep cleaning those bathrooms and scrubbing the kitchen floor require a dedicated morning. Again, all hands on deck! Your boys can and should learn how to scrub bathrooms. Your daughters need to know how to clean out a refrigerator, and your little boy needs to know how to wash the car inside and out. Starting young helps keep the momentum going and everyone is the better for it!

10. *Assign meals to a specific child.*

On busy days, I've said more than once, "Please cook dinner tonight. I don't care what it is—just google a recipe and make sure there's nutritious food on the table at 6:00." My girls turned out some fabulous dinners, often without a recipe. I had fun trying new dishes and they learned a lifelong skill, one their future roommates or families will be grateful for!

11. *Let go of expectations.*

It's OK if you purchase chopped onions and don't make your own cheese. (Yes, some mothers do that!) Cut corners and don't try to do everything. Relax so that you can be the very thing your family needs most of all. Most things we fret over simply are not worth our energy. *Not every little thing is big.* Breathe, and drink your coffee; let go and live a little!

Lord, help us to experience a life of peace where we know we're managing our time and doing what is best for ourselves and those around us. Help us cultivate ourselves and make life happen for us rather than to us. Give us wisdom in practical areas so our days have space for emotional and spiritual areas as well.

Day 29

Not that we dare to classify or compare ourselves with some of those who are commending themselves. But when they measure themselves by one another and compare themselves with one another, they are without understanding. (2 Corinthians 10:12, ESV)

There are plums to pit and freeze, an entire wheelbarrow plus three more containers of them. I teach the youngest his school, then stand at that outdoor table in the sunshine for two hours, nearly immobile but for my fingers flying as fast as possible, and my lips moving with instructions to bring the two middle kids through math.

A friend pulls in and takes some plums, then stays and helps me out. She's one of those people I love hanging with, and she doesn't mind that I'm a mess while she's all prettied up.

My five-year-old son hosts her daughter well, and they head inside to make themselves PB&J sandwiches. I tell the other kids to do the same, because I can't cook lunch today.

I find the ten-year-old upstairs with tears in his eyes, hovered over a gigantic science book. We sit, and we talk. This new co-op we joined suits the girls much better than him, and I tell him it's OK, he doesn't need Latin and technology-based writing.

He does need science and writing, but he can stick to something more basic. He wipes his eyes and feels better; so does Mama. It's OK that he's not interested in going to college. I can see who he's meant to be. The twelve-year-old downstairs with the articulate brain is getting a kick out of detailed computer discoveries. But this ten-year-old boy has a different life and calling ahead of him. He will get a great education, but he will do just fine without Latin.

Five o'clock hits again, and it's almost dinnertime.

The ten-year-old asks if he can make an apple pie. The thought of more mess drives me crazy so I talk him into a plum crisp instead. It turns out beautifully, and I ponder this boy.

Another friend comes by for plums. She's a kind soul, and we chat for a while. One more friend comes by, and she's a joy-filled person with a great big heart with enough room for all of us. She's fast becoming one of my favorites, because she's one of those down-to-earth women with no agenda but love. Someone called her a woman of valor the other day, and I agree.

We sit over a delicious meal, and we're all there, the friend, me, and my four. We haven't yet discovered all the answers to making our days simpler, but we know we will, and for now, Jamaican stir-fry, fresh kale salad, and plum crisp piled high with whipped cream is enough for the day.

Dinner is over, and the kids do their chores while I head for my favorite spot in the corner. It's strange how typing speedily can make the heart go quiet, calm, refreshed.

Each day has its own stresses, for sure, but when we're in those "I can't breathe" kind of places, something needs to give or we will end up losing. The same is true for our children.

Notice and celebrate who each child is rather than feeling bound to create each child to be who the world thinks they should be. Hear this—it's OK for your son not to want college and it's OK for your daughter to want it. It's OK not to do Latin for one child but to pursue more challenging lessons for another child.

More than fit a mold, children need to be accepted and grown right where they are.

The rest we learn to apply to our lives as mothers needs to be transferred right over to our children. Just as I didn't have to measure up to my friends, so my children don't need to measure up to each other.

It's up to me to notice their limitations and be OK with that. Then, it's up to me to help them be OK with that, too. Both of us have limits, which if exceeded, will drive us beyond goodness right into craziness.

Both our own and our children's physical or mental incapabilities are often God's way of showing us how to line up to His plan for our lives when we're pushing our own.

Father, help us not compare our children to each other, or ourselves to other mothers. Thank You for beautiful rest as we simply walk in all You've called us to.

Day 30

I love the Lord, because he has heard my voice and my pleas for mercy. Because he inclined his ear to me, therefore I will call on him as long as I live. (Psalm 116:1–2, ESV)

"Mama, we have to give a presentation on someone we admire, and I'm going to choose you!" The nine-year-old daughter glows.

Just this morning, this same girl got up on the wrong side of her bed and spent the morning yelling at her siblings. She had time-outs, but still got in the car with weepy eyes for her day at homeschool co-op.

I want to coddle her. What does she need most? How to know?

The other day the five-year-old was really frustrated and I found myself in the same dilemma. Some parents quench anger quickly with a hasty, "Hush, you shouldn't be angry" while others ask, "How are you feeling? Why are you feeling that way?"

Some adults vent feelings all the time but have little grace to overcome damaging emotions. Little discipline governs their lives. Others show little emotion or ability to connect with their spouse or friends, because they've never learned that people can be a safe place to find refuge even when their feelings are negative.

I want to raise children who are able to express their feelings well, but also rein them in if need be. I want to raise adults who can share their hearts with their spouses whether they are negative or positive, but who won't damage their own families with hurtful words and actions.

I stare at the frustrated son, and I ask, "Are you feeling frustrated? Do you feel helpless?" He nods his head, yes. He's incredibly frustrated.

"Is it because you don't know how to draw this barn?" I ask.

He nods again. He's a perfectionist, and taking a wild guess at architecture puts him into a panic.

"When you feel this way, son, you may tell Mama that you really don't know how, and you really do need help, but you don't need to yell or be frustrated. You can ask nicely." I sit beside him and draw a curve, then a line. He follows me, and soon we have a barn.

He nods his head to the frustration advice. He understands, and we move on.

I needed to train my daughter this morning, but he seems to need something different at the moment. Obedience is required, so when a child continues to disobey after talking it out, he needs consequences. But consequences need to come after a hearing of their hearts.

Hearing a child doesn't mean allowing him to rule the atmosphere with negative emotions; it simply means you hear the negative so you can better instill the positive.

Quickly shushing a child right up can close their hearts right up. Then, you might sit there wondering why the heart isn't open to receive.

We cannot only listen well when they feel "good" feelings; we must engage even more carefully when they feel anger, frustration, or fear. It is imperative to give them a safe place to share where they are heard, then gently guided.

Stuffing negative feelings allows them to fester and grow. Sharing them in a safe environment brings them to light, which allows them to diffuse more readily.

Rather than shutting frustration right up, we can ask, "Are you feeling frustrated? How can we come up with a solution for your problem?" Then, work to navigate for a good solution. This will teach your child that expressing a need brings a better result than lashing out or shutting down.

God is a God of light, and He wants us to show our kids how to walk into the light with their hearts.

You will have much fewer chances to walk your child through difficulty if you shut them down or scold them immediately when they express negative emotions.

If you don't listen, but respond to all negative emotions with a scolding, telling them they shouldn't feel this way, they will most likely become adults who have difficulty connecting with others in a close, transparent way.

If a child is raised having good connections only when their emotions are "in line," they will likely perform for their spouse and others in order to gain love and approval.

My son didn't need discipline; he needed me to hear him, and he responded well. The nine-year-old daughter didn't respond well, but continued lashing her way through the morning. She needed consequences.

If all you do is ask questions and listen, your child will run over you, and your home will be chaotic. You will be at your wit's end most of the time. Your child will test you to the end of your ability to stay calm, and then, you will probably snap and yell right back.

If all you do is give consequences for negative reactions and emotions, your child will probably learn to perform for approval. He will retreat into a room by himself when he's in need rather than open his heart to you. And he will most likely grow to be an adult who feels alone.

Learn to listen well, ask questions, walk them through—and only give consequences when deliberate disobedience after all that calls for it.

Lord Jesus, thank You that You've inclined Your ear to us. There's nothing You don't understand about us, and there's nothing You don't have time to listen to. Help us truly understand our children and live all of life from that premise of love.

Day 31

And because lawlessness will be increased, the love of many will grow cold.
But the one who endures to the end will be saved.
And this gospel of the kingdom will be proclaimed throughout the whole world as a testimony to all nations, and then the end will come.
(Matthew 24:12–14 ESV)

I remember how close I came to death, how hard I fought, how long I waited until the blood flow stopped when my third baby was born. When the trickle finally stopped, we knew I would survive.

Some of the most dangerous influences are subtle, just as some of the most dangerous bleeding is slow but steady. Life drifts away from the body so slowly and quietly that we don't notice because we see no gush of red. Ironically, a trickle of blood can be more dangerous than a gush because we don't see what's happening.

I was close to death but didn't feel it.

The same thing can happen in our spiritual lives. Believers spend so much time on television or social media that there is little time for the Word. People are more ready to be distant than live in community because there is always the screen to turn on, the opportunity to be mesmerized, transported to another world.

We don't really need each other anymore. Or we don't think we do.

The more time we spend drenching our lives with shows and social media, the more we are influenced. Believers may say they are not, that they learn from these things, but many hours spent weekly watching darkness does, of necessity, eat up your time with darkness of the world rather than the light of Christ.

We already know evil is here. What are we doing to permeate it with light?

Why saturate our minds and take up hours of our time with it, daily? How many hours do we waste when we could be growing ourselves and those around us?

We can't raise our kids saturated in the world, then ask them not to follow it when they are teens. We must give them something better, higher, more meaningful to soak up their attention.

"You shall make no covenant with them . . . for they would turn away your sons from following me, to serve other Gods" (Deuteronomy 7:2b & 4 ESV).

"For you are a people holy to the Lord your God" (Deuteronomy 7:5–6a ESV).

In the twenty-first century there may not be carved images to break, but idols of the heart. Our daughters quickly apply Hollywood standards of popularity and beauty to their own lives unless they are guided to better.

Our sons watch shows that promote manhood by how many girls they can get to bed, unless they see a real man loving a woman who, most likely, doesn't look like any of the girls on the show.

If kids are constantly watching shows where the main character is sassy and gets his own way, they will most likely adopt the same attitudes. If a teen or adult constantly watches shows with immorality and violence, they will become more immune to it.

In the same way, when we feed ourselves and our kids good, we will grow and be changed by it. Purchase good books, take your children to classes and groups where they will hear good, see good, and live alongside others who value truth.

Already, we are pressed for time. Already, Christ asks us to pray that there would be laborers sent into His harvest.

How can we harvest good when we sow the bad just as much as, or more, than the good?

Lord Jesus, help us to be taken with light, life, and kingdom purpose. Help us feed the same to our children so they see beauty more than ugly, life more than death, and goodness more than evil.

DAY 32

Therefore, my beloved brothers, be steadfast, immovable, always abounding in the work of the Lord, knowing that in the Lord your labor is not in vain. (1 Corinthians 15:58, ESV)

A slight form stumbled into my room in the dead of night, and all he could do was say he needed something.

Sure enough, there it was again—that dreaded smell saturated his clothes and bed with icky wetness. I cleaned and wiped and comforted yet again.

He stared at the wipe container. "Mama, just look at that baby. Her smile is so annoying. Just look at her. It is so annoying when babies smile like that."

I see the model child's grinning little face and know it must appear to him like she's smiling jubilantly with no regard for his nighttime suffering. I tuck him on the couch, but in a short while he's crawling into bed with me, and the rest of my night is spent trying to sleep while feeling smothered.

He rises bright and early. "Mama, do you know why I slept in your bed? Because we just bought the couch and I didn't want to make a mess on it."

Apparently he didn't realize I'd much rather clean a leather couch than my mattress.

I pull the wet, smelly sheets off his bed, but we are out of laundry soap.

I go to fry eggs, but they're still out in the car from a few days ago.

I go to take the trash out, and the garbage can is all the way out by the road.

Then, I reach for the cream, but it, too, was hiding in the minivan covered in coats still remaining from the weekend. At least it was cold enough outside to keep it from spoiling.

The creamy coffee warms my throat, and for a few minutes all seems well again. Then the neighbor lady calls. She's had a leak in her rental, carpenters have left a load of dust everywhere, and her renter is upset. Could I clean at short notice?

I drive over and enter a lovely little home occupied by a distraught bachelor who is unnerved with the chaos. I vacuum, scrub toilets, wipe counters—and he talks.

He's just been retired and his prominent job of thirty-four years is behind him. He doesn't know how long he will stay in the house on the bay, though he loves it. Perhaps he will live in South America for a while just to see what it would be like.

I stare at the waves lapping the shore. The windows afford such a view, it seems as if I'm right above the water. It's breathtaking, but affords him little pleasure. The waters seem morose and silent, unlike the usual beauty I feel beckoning my soul.

His words sound hollow, empty. *He has it all, but is still not sure of his joy.* I look around and notice books on how to cultivate joy.

Doesn't he have what we are all striving for—a quiet, well-financed life in the older years, surrounded with beauty and endless options? But he's still seeking joy.

How can one work many years for retirement, then feel restless when it comes? How can one work so diligently without more reward for the heart when it's over?

I drove home to the little green house full of laundry, dishes, and schoolbooks. We ate leftovers and browsed Pinterest for some cute fall photo shoot ideas. But I realized the joy I felt wasn't so much in the actual pictures we would get, but in the time spent together brainstorming.

Because the best things in life will never be things.

Invest in people. Invest in them even while the home is a mess. Invest in them far more than you ever invest in things.

Allow the days to wing by without perfection.

Expect a mess.

Anticipate needing to settle squabbles.

Put your phone away (hide it, if need be).

Sit on the bed with a child just to talk.

Always kiss each child goodnight.

Adjust your spending habits so you can afford time at home with your kids. Buy an inexpensive car, shop in bulk, live in a simpler house.

Shop less at Christmastime and spend the extra time baking with your kids. Read them the real Jesus story and let them see its impact on your life.

Learn to be happy in a mess.

Learn to relax before the day is over.

Living like this will ensure less time for "things." But the foundation of your home will be rooted in love, which makes all things of importance grow well.

Our hearts are created to absorb something greater than material possessions.

This is why things don't satisfy and why we need to be caught up in the great story of Christ, be wrapped up in His plans, be life givers and love bearers to those He loves.

If He gave His life for people, doesn't He want us to give our time and energy to love?

Let the body grow old, but let the soul become rich. It begins now, here, today. Let the posture of your heart be one of going all out for people—not things—and the years will unfold with more riches.

Rather than view each day as a destination to reach, view it as a gift, as an open book where you get to fill the pages with story—not with how much work you've gotten accomplished but with how many hearts you've gotten to hold.

If you live this way, Mama, you have nothing to fear when seasons change. Each season will bring its own difficulties, but you will ride them with grace, thankful for the good in all of them.

Lord Jesus, thank You that our souls were never meant to be satisfied with things, but with Your Person. From that premise, help us love on Your people, especially our families.

DAY 33

And the King will answer them, "Truly, I say to you, as you did it to one of the least of these my brothers, you did it to me." (Matthew 25:40, ESV)

December winged right in, and *I was rocking it.*

Making truffles was high on my priority list for some reason, and more days than one found me in the kitchen squishing Oreos and cream cheese together before shaping them into bite-sized balls ready to be coated in melted chocolate.

White elephant parties coming right up had me roaming the aisles for some meaningful gift some person would actually want to keep.

Amazon came to my rescue in the family gift-giving department, and because we don't buy many toys for the kids, purchasing Legos and rockets for the five-year-old was true joy.

Homemade rolls were baked and gifted to the neighbors, and all those distant relatives had photo cards coming in the mail.

I was having fun, but I was stressed. My head felt thick and my body exhausted, and I couldn't for the life of me understand why I felt like crying when I was having fun. But the pressure of so much to do rolled and swirled in my head, and when the kids had one more spat I felt like I might lose my mind.

How on earth does a mother homeschool and still reach out to all the people she wants to? I found myself patting the kids good night quickly before descending the stairs in hopes of a few quiet moments before exhaustion forced my eyes closed. Though really I would have rather read for an hour because in all the hubbub my heart needs to be fed and my mind wants to engage at least a little.

But I missed sitting with the kids at their bedsides, rubbing backs and singing into ears nearly tuned out to all noise at the entrance of oblivion. And I missed talking with God.

I found myself wondering if I really needed an early Sunday morning at church to connect deeply with Christ. And then it hit me: good things were robbing me of the best things.

I chat with a friend, and she tells me how she wants to buy for this person and that one, but forces herself to stop. She's great at slowing down. And I learn from her that radiance doesn't happen when the heart, soul, and body are constantly drained.

Will my family, friends, and neighbors benefit more from a plate of homemade goodness, or from the goodness permeating my soul when I engage with them?

If I focus on doing all things good, it can take away from being all things good, like love, joy, and peace. Like being rested enough to engage with others meaningfully. Like having the mental capacity to listen and learn and deal with these four little people with four different levels of need and desire.

I see mothers just like me running, running, running.

Somehow we feel less than, left behind, leftover when we're not accomplishing all these things.

Can the daughter learn enough dance from one lesson a week rather than two? She begs to go—her friends are going. I stop a moment, then pause a full ten minutes to explain how life can be so full that the heart ceases to be full—and we're at that point.

For once in my life, I have the courage to say "no," and really mean it.

Dancing is awesome, sports can be fun, gifting things over Christmastime to those we love can be meaningful, but let's get this—*there's nothing meaningful that isn't done with love.*

Love has nothing to do with stress. Love has nothing to do with accomplishments and being as "well-equipped" for life as the Joneses.

Kids who rush about, performing for others, can end up with hearts dead to service, kindness, humility, and compassion. Mothers who rush about accommodating it all can end up with hearts dead to living, breathing, vibrant Life.

I slow down, right in the month of December. I pack up the son and head to the gym, let him play while I ease the stress by lifting weights and running on the tread mill. Later, we all swim, then have a slumber party by the Christmas tree while I read the story of Jesus's birth in the dimly lit, glowing house. The dog slumbers by the door and the boys lean in for a hug. We slowed down right in the middle of the mess.

Refreshing rest leads to more productive seasons. Because when you exhale, you create more air in your lungs to inhale. Just as we need to both inhale and exhale air to breathe properly—and therefore, stay alive—so we need to both rest and work.

The kids need quiet stories of Christ read to them in their mama's presence more than they need another sport, more dance lessons, or another play date. They grow up soon enough, and the world will always be there. Mama won't always be there when the world and its pressures speak to their hearts daily, luring them in.

Has Mama lured them in with peace, knowledge of Christ, and spiritual nurture? Or has Mama kept such a steady pace with the world that her kids have seriously lacked any semblance of other worldliness?

Have their days been so full of action that they haven't seen the acts of Christ?

Does your teenage daughter know how to perform more than she knows how to serve?

Does your son know how to push his way around on the football field more than he knows how to pull others along in strong but kind leadership?

If we're so busy accomplishing, we have few moments left to serve a sick mother together, help out when a family is in need, or visit the elderly. We're so busy doing that we end up doing little in the name of true love.

Get this, mothers—God is far more interested that your children learn to serve others than He is in them winning awards for dance performances or sports teams. Just as you carve out time for yourselves, you need to carve out time in their schedules so that together, you can say yes to that widow needing her wood stacked or that new mother needing a meal.

I remember the day I told my young teen daughter that we would be joining our church in handing out flyers to the town even though her friend was coming over. Her friend joined us that day, and though it wasn't what they wanted at first, we learned about values that day. *Teach your children to serve by making time to serve.*

God tells us, right here and now in modern day America where self-expression and self-development are often idolized, that true religion is found in this way of life—to visit the fatherless and the widows (James 1:27).

He tells us that when we do things for the needy, we do it for Him—rather, *unto Him.*

Tomorrow, how about you enter the kitchen with your daughter and have her bake some muffins for that sick mama down the road while you stir up a big pot of chili? Together, you deliver it. How about you send your son to help the widow with her firewood—and tell her the labor is free?

Lord, we know that Christmas gifts are good—but the ultimate gift of Christmastime is Love.

Day 34

Strength and dignity are her clothing, and she laughs at the time to come. She opens her mouth with wisdom, and the teaching of kindness is on her tongue. She looks well to the ways of her household and does not eat the bread of idleness. Her children rise up and call her blessed. (Proverbs 31:25–28a, ESV)

It's New Year, and I ask myself: "Do you have any big goals for the year?"

I think back to my drive home from town the other day when the children and I discussed my life, and what I do. I tried to show them how deeply I value being their mother as we discussed careers, mothering, and what it means to be a woman.

Motherhood is in question these days. Many women feel incompetent if they aren't out making money or building a career.

Some of us need to earn a living whether we want to or not. Yet, all of us are called to bring the best to our homes whenever possible. If no one cooks the food, cleans the toilet, decorates the home, and provides a warm atmosphere for the kids and others, who will?

When I hear women say, "I'm just a stay-at-home mom," I cringe. *Just?*

If mothers get to be home with their babies while enjoying each developing year, they hold in their hands a gift greater than anything money could buy.

If we're this negative about mothering, why would our daughters want to grow up doing the same thing we did?

I'm not opposed to working moms when the need is there. I have to work, also. But mothering is always of greater importance than a career. It is not lowly to stay home with your children!

Today I sat with two other mothers while our kids ran wild in the snow. Two fathers took them to the road and watched while they safely zoomed down the hill. They were red cheeked, exhausted, and happy while we sat discussing our lives as women. They were entirely committed, happy moms and it was refreshing to sit with women unafraid and unabashedly proud of what they do.

I could see it in the kids. These are some of the most polite, kind, well-adjusted kids I know. They treat others with respect, work hard, play hard, love others, and serve well. These kids are golden.

Their parents don't depend on church or Sunday school to bring Christ into their hearts. They're not always running to every sport or function, but have many peaceful days at home learning what kids need to learn.

All because Mama is willing to be Mama and considers that her chief prerogative. Even as she sits there with a sprained ankle and messy house full of guests, and her husband serves peanut butter and jelly to the kids.

I sit by the wood fire eating leftover popcorn, and I muse on the gift she's given us just by being her. She's readily available to have us over because she's not fretting over a nice dinner or perfect home. I walk into her house relieved and genuinely blessed to eat stale popcorn and dip hot chocolate from the massive pot simmering on the stove. And then, I sprawl out on the floor in front of the woodstove and soak it all in.

My kids have been running to this and that, and I've felt stressed, tense, and burnt out. When we made it home, I sat them down and explained to them my goal for the beginning of the year. We would be slowing down and staying home more.

My son whispers in my ear, "Mama, I like what you're saying. I'd love to have more time to do things together. We are often so rushed even when we do get to do things."

I hold him close. When you do too many things, you end up doing well in none. Kids need peace, schedule, discipline, and fun. How can Mama provide any of it if she's always running?

At the end of our lives, what we accomplish will mean far less than the love we grew with our children.

The other two mothers advise me, "Learn to say no. You don't need to raise someone else's child, or always be there for everyone. You need to be there for your kids while they are still with you."

I haven't been present enough because I've been stressed trying to keep people loved and happy. Good grief. Even with four, it's easy to feel like just being with them isn't quite enough. I should be able to do more, be more, accomplish more.

"Write down all you're doing, and you will see that you're doing enough," they say. And my eyes well up in tears of gratefulness to these wise women. They are as strong, competent, and capable as any career woman. (Don't many career women even say that staying home is more difficult than working?)

No one praises you for changing diapers, grading math books, or packing a lunch. The world high-fives women who have titles to their name or degrees to show. Working the corporate ladder offers promotional possibilities and high respect from coworkers. Even your boss may be more appreciative and verbally thankful than your family at home.

Which feels better, wearing heels and being verbally acknowledged by your company for your hard work, or giving yourself to your kids all day without a word of thanks? Which is easier? Which calls for more sacrifice?

These are the reasons motherhood needs to be held in high honor. Those who give much, gain much.

If all kids were raised well, the world would change. And more kids could be raised in exemplary fashion if mamas would embrace the nobility of their calling.

Whether you need to work or you're able to stay home, refuse to label yourself anything less than the noble title you own in motherhood. Hold it in high esteem. Brush your hair, stay healthy, and hold your head high when you walk those grocery aisles with children in tow.

Make the world think twice before degrading motherhood by wearing your badge with honor and dignity.

Father, thank You that You are my Father, and Your approval is the one I care about most. Help me value mothering as You do, and place it as priority over all other career opportunities.

DAY 35

But I discipline my body and keep it under control, lest after preaching to others I myself should be disqualified. (1 Corinthians 9:27, ESV)

Today, let's tackle a few things our families may wish to mention but refuse to because they're too kind (or don't want to get in trouble!).

Woman to woman, we're good at making excuses. These excuses can bog us down for many years. Let's take a look at just a few:

"I'm a mom, so I get to be overweight."

"I'm a stay-at-home mom, so I don't need to cultivate my mind."

"I'm a mom and it takes all my time, so I won't utilize my talents."

We become aimless and rather than make our time purposeful, we get lost in the shuffle. We grab the phone and scroll through our newsfeeds rather than take that fifteen minutes to get on with something of value that we never have time for. (Fifteen minutes a day adds up to many hours at the end of the year.)

We are moms, but guess what?

Even learning one new thing a day will refresh and engage the part of your brain that feels dormant in these child-rearing years. With Google at our fingertips, we can learn one new thing in less than two minutes.

Purposeful parenting may mean we give the kids some downtime on purpose so we can do our thing.

It means we take time with the kids on purpose, as well.

We're moms, but perhaps one of our goals could be getting through more good books rather than spending as much time on Facebook.

Perhaps we could choose health rather than indulgence, and actually feel good about ourselves.

If we have great big goals, we can make baby steps toward those goals while we're raising our children.

The goal is not perfection, it is growth. Always forward!

We don't need to live apathetic lives just because we're prioritizing our kids. Our minds and bodies still need to be cared for and improved, and those desires we have to reach beyond the walls of our homes may be there because God has something for us to do.

During those precious moments of free time, reach for your goals. It will keep you alive and fresh, with vision and excitement for life.

Don't waste your time; use it.

Pick up your weights, grab your pen, or order that book.

If there's no time even for that, try that nutritious way of eating and push your babies in a double stroller with a smile and a quick step.

When I had three babies in a little over three years (and very little money to spend), I bought a used double stroller and walked through town. Many evenings after dinner was made I put the two youngest in the stroller and had my three-year-old walk after me a few blocks.

My mind and body needed to get active. Lifting even the third child into the stroller and pushing it up a very steep hill allowed me to get the exercise I needed when there was no time or money for a gym membership.

Mothers, we can use what we have to do what we can do. Even in that little apartment in town (I'm an outdoorsy girl to the core), there was a choice—get depressed and lazy, or get walking and healthy.

In every stage of life, no matter the circumstances of our life, we get to choose what kind of women we are.

Woman to woman, I'm urging us moms to be inspired and inspiring in both our mental state and our physical well-being!

Lord, help us be good stewards of our bodies. Thank You for Your good heart toward Your daughters. You never intended us to get permanently unhealthy from bearing children. Help us to make wise choices that align us to Your plan for our bodies.

DAY 36

Let it be so now, for thus it is fitting for us to fulfill all righteousness.
(Matthew 3:15, ESV)

"I don't have time for quiet time," I heard her say.

It's OK, I thought. *All day can be spent with Jesus because He is always with us.*

Mornings begun in a haste over breakfast, school, and beds can be just as holy as time in the Word and prayer. You may feel frustrated because you want to tune in. ***Know in such times that tuning in to your family's needs is tuning in to the Lord.***

Don't resent stirring that pot of oatmeal first thing in the morning.

Know that in keeping your home well, you equip hearts well, and the world needs well-kept hearts.

In building up your home, you build the world. Because when homes break, society breaks right along with them.

Allow yourself to be broken and given so the world can be whole.

Mothering is not so much about cleaning, cooking, and laundry as it is about hearts. Hearts know love when the atmosphere speaks goodness and peace, with needs noticed and met.

When mealtimes come, make sure there's food available, and plenty of it.

At bedtime, read Scripture over little minds and pray around the circle. Who better to teach them how to pray than their own mother (or father)?

Place your cell phone on a high shelf so you're not reaching for it every thirty minutes.

Look into the eyes of your child, and gaze even more into their hearts.

We are not stuck in a mindless routine; we are master builders.

We're not victims of constant chaos; we are navigators.

We need not become dull and lifeless; we are shaping lives, and thus society.

If you're trying to force something different (*bigger* or *greater)* to happen, it's not meant to be yours—at least not yet. If you're grabbing at something to the harm of those around you, you're meant to release it.

If it's meant to be yours, God will show you a way to do it without damaging those around you or depriving them of what they need.

Do your best, walk patiently, live fully; make the most of your time, and life will unfold. You have only to be faithful. Some of the best things in life will come your way when you make wise choices in smaller areas. This is faithfulness, this is stewardship, this is tapping in to your talents and gifts in all the ways you can without damaging or depriving those around you.

Never take on a religious persona of doing something for God, while rejecting the peace of God for yourself and those around you.

With everything that comes to us in a day, may this be our heart of acceptance.

Father, thank You that my time with You can be all through the day. Thank You that my relationship with You is not based on what I do in the morning, but by seeing what You want to do throughout the day, and partnering with You in it. Help me be at rest in my spirit when my home is active and I long for quiet.

Day 37

She has done what she could. (Mark 14:8, ESV)

Newton's third law of motion states that for every action, there is an equal and opposite reaction.

That's a bit how I felt when I watched the house turn to shambles after cleaning it for a few hours. Each thing I did to make our home a lovely, welcoming place was undone with the strength of four others. And I was overwhelmed with more than I could possibly do in the moments I had.

When Mary poured out the alabaster box of ointment on Jesus's feet, Jesus praised her for it and said, "She did what she could." Not only that, but He mentioned that everywhere the gospel is preached, her deed will be remembered.

He was right. Many centuries later, this mama is breathing in His words. I'm learning from Jesus's own statement of approval, "She has done what she could."

Jesus never asked us to give until we are fallen over in a heap of exhaustion because we ran ourselves ragged trying to help. He knew the poor were there, and mentioned that they would always be there—but He wouldn't be. He saw the momentary need, her heart of gold for that precise action.

He never told her to go do something else. He wanted her to live the moment He placed on her heart. This was her time to break that expensive box of ointment and pour it over His head in love and worship.

This moment and you. This is your time whether it's giving in to the joy of a dream, serving your children, or loving someone in need. This is your moment to do what you can.

Jesus expects nothing more or less of you.

Don't ignore a need when you are able to reach in. Don't silence your heart just because you're not able to do something like start an organization or lead a ministry. Do what you can.

Jesus silenced Mary's accusers with truth—the truth that "She has done what she could."

Her small moment, though not reaching the world of the poor, touched His heart so greatly that He wanted it mentioned through many centuries of gospel preaching.

Mary didn't berate herself for not reaching more people. Nor did she hold back on what was in her heart to do because she felt like it wasn't big enough. Mary embraced the moment—she did what she could—and she made glad the Son of Man.

What can you do? What is your moment?

Newton's third law of motion seems to apply to mothers. For every action we do, there seems to be an opposite reaction of equal strength, undoing what we've just accomplished.

When we learn to live in a single moment and do what we can, we find the blessing of heaven on our efforts and they are multiplied. This is the key to avoiding exhaustion and condemnation for not doing more, more, and more.

Galatians 3:3 (ESV) asks, "Having begun by the Spirit, are you now being perfected by the flesh?" Mothers, rather than struggling to accomplish all things, we must focus on the One thing—Jesus. He will lead you; He will guide you into the life you long for as you do what you can in each moment He gives you.

Whether your moment means living it up with the kids, or breaking the ointment over Jesus's head in worship on your kitchen floor, or simply cooking another meal for those wonderful people you get to love on each day—simply make it your moment and do what you can.

Father, thank You that You love me just as much when I can't fit in down time as You do when I spend an hour with You in the morning. Thank You that Your love is not based on performance. Thank You that You're with me all day, every day, no matter what.

Day 38

Be still, and know that I am God. I will be exalted among the nations, I will be exalted in the earth! (Psalm 46:10, ESV)

I picked up the book.

Pride and Prejudice fascinated me with its long, wordy paragraphs. Watching the movie had brought much joy and laughter to my life, but I had never read Jane Austen's books. I couldn't quite get past the lengthy style of script.

I'm struck today as I see the difference in books from 1813 to 2020. Today, paragraphs are less lengthy to keep the reader engaged. And aside from books, we're scrolling through media with swift swipes of the hand, engaged in one thing after another at lightning speed.

Because we're so accustomed to the fast, easy, entertaining world, we're less prone to click on links of noteworthy thought and serious engagement. If we're not careful, we lose out on rich soul food while we feast on eye candy.

I'm sitting at Barnes & Noble today with my friend, watching her sign another copy of her lovely book, and I'm struck with the vast amount of stuff we have to occupy our minds. It's becoming more and more difficult to grab and engage people's attention because everyone is already bombarded.

Like this!

Follow my page!

Subscribe to my channel!

Buy my book!

And the ever-present, "What? You haven't seen *that* movie?"

The world is literally begging for the absorption of our kids' minds, time, and thought.

Mothers, we are either blocking the way to God or we are preparing the way to God. Those things we think are neither here nor there are a means to leading our kids either there, or here.

Our kids are growing up in a postmodern world with many, many distractions. Thought of any depth is disintegrating while its replacement of flashing screens, video games, and iPhones so occupy the minds of growing kids that there is little room left.

Who wants a good book with uplifting morals when there are gripping, riveting movies to watch? Problem is, much of the excitement we place before our kids involves little that is moral, and therefore reduces the value of morality as its lack is glorified in the stories our kids grow to love.

Our kids lose vision because of this. What occupies their days ends up grabbing their hearts.

We were born to crave greater things than ourselves. Rather than ask your children not to crave, give them something better to satisfy their cravings.

Never shut down a child; simply redirect him.

Never spiritualize things so greatly that there is no room for human thought and feeling—simply teach your child to bring his passions under the control of Christ.

Forbidding passion will shut down a child; redirecting passion will bring life to your child.

We can't rewind history and throw iPhones into outer space, but we can and must teach our children where the deepest longings of their hearts can be met. This is our great privilege as mothers!

And while we can't rewind culture and rid society of certain things, we can redirect our children to the God who is over and above all things. We can show them what it looks like to live with passion and joy under the guidance of a heavenly Father, the very One we were made to crave.

Father, help us enjoy the mental quietness You offer us, and help us be faithful to bring that to our children. Help us keep their passion for life alive while showing them how to direct their passion toward You most of all.

Day 39

Do not be conformed to this world, but be transformed by the renewal of your mind, that by testing you may discern what is the will of God, what is good and acceptable and perfect. (Romans 12:2, ESV)

Our kids are not growing up in a quiet world of nature and value as children did in previous generations. They are surrounded with constant noise and infiltration of people, places, and things that kids a few decades ago never needed to navigate.

The simple practice of handing our kids iPhones allows them to be in another world. Never before have kids been involved in so many peoples' lives in a single day. This distraction alone can lead them away from peaceful living to constant interruption.

Our kids' minds are becoming restless with normal living. Creativity and family time grow scarce as heads are bent over screens. *Being in touch with the world at large can cause us to be out of touch with the world around us.*

Phones are carried to bedrooms at night, where they are held in the hand until sleep takes over. Teens fall asleep wondering how many likes their selfie got that day rather than reading a good book, leading them closer to a good Creator God with a vision much broader than themselves.

The heart is created for largeness, and that craving can't be met on a screen.

In our postmodern world, this thirst for something greater than ourselves is often sought to be met with dramatization flashing before us on a screen rather than actually living something great, for Someone great.

Reality ceases to thrill us when we are absorbed with unrealistic actions in overproportioned quantities. Our minds become dull unless they are activated time and again with the same thrill. This becomes an addiction, and our lives are changed slowly from the inside out as our hearts become immune to sin and too distracted to absorb the things of Christ.

Give a child a stick and a rope to play with, and they will create something fun. Sit him constantly in front of dramatized shows, and he will be dull and lifeless unless he has another show to thrill him.

Give a child constant access to screens, phones, and video games, and he may absorb the world he sees rather than the Christ who is not seen, but felt with the heart.

Our swift addiction to these things is merely a reminder of the heart's quest for something larger than itself. When we become absorbed with snapping selfies, videoing ourselves for TikTok, or photographing each thing we do, we lose out on the wonder of living. We were never meant to be so into ourselves for the sake of ourselves.

There's a grander picture. Our hearts are created to crave and know greater capacity. And it's up to us mothers to lead them to the greatness they were born to crave by showing them the wonder of Jesus Christ and actively pulling goodness into their lives in every way possible. This is done best, not by focusing on how bad things are, but by celebrating and pulling in the good.

Father, thank You for creating us to crave You. Lead us to Yourself, and draw our children close to Your heart as they see You in those around them.

Day 40

I charge you in the presence of God and of Christ Jesus, who is to judge the living and the dead, and by his appearing and his kingdom:

Preach the word; be ready in season and out of season; reprove, rebuke, and exhort, with complete patience and teaching.

For the time is coming when people will not endure sound teaching, but having itching ears they will accumulate for themselves teachers to suit their own passions, and will turn away from listening to the truth and wander off into myths.

As for you, always be sober-minded, endure suffering, do the work of an evangelist, fulfill your ministry. (2 Timothy 4:1–5, ESV)

Sometimes our minds unknowingly long for the rest of bygone days when we didn't need to keep up with hundreds of different people and could focus on the handful right before us.

We enjoyed each other more in those days. We laughed more, had more meaningful conversations, spent more time together.

In the not-so-distant past, no one had the TV to rush home to after church. People looked to each other for company more than they sought the next show for entertainment.

Our world is changing from the inside out, subtly, slowly, but certainly.

Mothers, never, ever hesitate to go against the flow of society so you can create space to foster hunger and capacity for the deeper things of life, love, and God.

Host others in your home, bring them in, and have your kitchen table be a welcoming place for all to be fed.

Teach your kids about different worldviews. Talk to them about Islam, New Spirituality, Marxism, Secularism, and Postmodernism. Teach them about the ever-pervasive views against government, authority, and institution, which fight against leadership but have no valuable alternative to replace it.

Teach them the true meaning of anarchy, and the resulting mayhem. Lead them to something higher than themselves by teaching them the value of authority at a young age.

By training your child at a young age, you are steering him to something higher than himself. You are paving the way to God. You are allowing him to enter teen years with a vision already grasped of his good place in a great, wide cosmos much larger than himself. He may still struggle in his teens, but he will have a foundation under his belt to remember.

You are giving him capacity to think beyond himself for the good of others, for the lifting up of true values, for the goodness of God more than the libertarian's unwavering promotion of self-interest.

Talk to your children about Darwinism. Don't leave them wondering when they hit the teen years and all the questions pile on at once while they are drenched in a humanistic, secular world with values diminishing at an astonishing rate even in the church.

Build a foundation, one strong and true. Let them know they were *created on purpose, not chanced by accident.* Teach Genesis thoroughly enough so they know it takes more faith to believe in the correct four or five cells merging at just the right time to chance them into existence than a good God creating them *on purpose for a good purpose.*

Grab hold of simple apologetics so you can teach your child the whys of what you believe. Never, ever expect your child to grow up accepting your beliefs without knowing the whys of your beliefs. If you do, the world will give him explanations for his questions while he has none of his own.

You must trump lesser thoughts in his mind with powerful truth, long before he reaches college. Begin young, and never stop.

I believe 2 Timothy 4:1–5 speaks directly to us as mothers, yet many of us leave most of the work of teaching our kids to pastors. Get this—kids will never learn all they need from a church service. You, Mother, are one of their greatest teachers.

Father, forgive us mothers for hiding behind dishes and diapers, allowing our minds to become dull and vacant. Help us realize the huge calling on our lives as we live days with our children and are one of their greatest influencers.

Day 41

But in your hearts honor Christ the Lord as holy, always being prepared to make a defense to anyone who asks you for a reason for the hope that is in you. (1 Peter 3:15, ESV)

My son sat on my bed late one night as I was finishing up a movie and asked, "Mom, do you want to talk?"

I paused the movie. Of course I wanted to catch up with this child.

We decided to share three highs and three lows of our day, then share a bit of wisdom we learned through it. I shared first, then he.

It struck me, this parenting dance—and how we're in season during the least expected hours while we're out of season during times we want them most. But what matters most is that we're *ready*.

If I hadn't learned and applied wisdom to my day, I would have had little to share. But God was on the move in my heart, and there were things on the tip of my tongue to share. What's more, it was so practical that even a teenage boy could relate to it.

He hadn't been home earlier, but he was chatting with me now. And I learned once more to take the moments I'm given rather than force the life I want.

Mothers, we are to be ready in and out of season. Our in-season happens while they are with us, sitting at our kitchen table or relaxing on our couches before bed.

If mothers realized the importance of being equipped to teach their kids, they would download teaching apps on their iPhones right along with Pinterest and Facebook apps. They would grab books and make truth priority, knowing that lies move in quickly when truth has no grounded place.

Plant truth in your child by filling your own soul with truth. When or if your child has seasons or even years of doubt, these truths will always surface to remind his heart of the way, truth, and life.

Talk to your kids about basic things, such as Genesis One's account of creation. Don't stop by reading the chapter and expecting them to accept it. Teach them the real difference between creation and evolution by backing it up with simple facts.

"Did you know that Mt. St. Helens' eruption created layers in three hours that evolutionists claim to take billions of years to form in other places?"

"Why do you think we are finding fossils of animals fully developed rather than fossils of evolving species? Don't you think that if species truly evolved, there would be fossils of different phases of fish rather than only of fish as they are today?"

Many Christians claim an evolutionistic approach to the creation story while saying it makes no difference to the gospel. Truth is, when we alter the foundation of what the gospel is based on, we water down the gospel. If the first chapter of the Bible isn't true, why would the rest be?

You cannot take away part of the word of God without weakening all the Words of God.

These are only small examples of the ways you can guide your child and give him shoes for the path he needs to walk. As your child grows older, there are endless resources you can integrate into your days right along with math, grammar, and science.

Let him already have owned his purpose and beliefs when he reaches the age where all kids grasp for meaning and identity.

Remove the constant texting, and begin studying, then talking. You won't talk to your kids when you're already on overload with texting fifty friends throughout the day. Raise your kids with fewer distractions so they have energy and desire for deeper things.

Allow them to see you taken with Christ and moving with His Spirit. Allow them to sense your excitement over His works, and leaning into your part of His greater-than-yourself story.

Lord Jesus, thank You that You are the way, the truth, and the life. Help us to fully engage our seasons of raising children. Give us grace to be there when they come to us. Give us even more grace to engage our hearts and minds into truths we can then translate for our children. We ask You for wisdom, and we thank You for it.

Day 42

As for the rich in this present age, charge them not to be haughty, nor to set their hopes on the uncertainty of riches, but on God, who richly provides us with everything to enjoy. (1 Timothy 6:17, ESV)

Watching my little boy jump from the trampoline into the pool was the best part of my day.

I had scoured Facebook Marketplace for both a trampoline and a pool, found both, and set them up long before the hottest days of summer hit. Moving to the South meant a lot of change, and the children needed more than a little house in a development after leaving everything behind in the West.

Most parents don't want their kids on screens all the time, but in order to be most effective in our approach, we need to replace a "no" with a "yes."

I can walk out the door to work at the coffeehouse alone, or I can invite my child to join me there with his own laptop and toys. He can do math across the table and I can end the day early to play a new game with him. The goal is to occupy his days with good things.

You can't say no to hours of screen time unless you also say yes to hours of active fun time. You can't harp constantly on what is wrong with the world unless you actively engage in what's right with the world, too.

You must keep the hearts of your kids more with the presence of good than with avoiding evil. Good overtakes the soul and makes life so rich that they have less need to engage in the evil.

You can't deprive your kids of what their peers do unless you also make sure they thrive with other things. Kids who grow up hearing "no" also need to grow up hearing many, many yeses. It's well worth investing in active playthings if you'll diminish screen entertainment.

When you steer your kids away from one thing, please be sure that you lead them toward another thing. Fill their lives with so much good that they are unaware of missing out on the negative. This is not to imply you always have to entertain them; it is good for children to entertain themselves.

When my oldest children were young, a tiny apartment didn't allow for many toys. We shared a yard with other families, and it was small. But they created their own fun with the few toys they had, and it was amazing to watch.

Make their lives happy, not so much by always entertaining them, but by providing things with which they can entertain themselves.

Invest in what they love. The secret to successful denial of one thing is to successfully grant them other things.

Your kids should not identify with the word *deprivation*; they should know the words *engagement* and *enjoyment*. Sacrifice your own pleasure for the well-being of your kids, and you will be richly rewarded.

Most parents work for forty hours a week, sleep for fifty-six, and have seventy-two hours left over for other things. That's a lot of hours! Plan your time, schedule fun things as you schedule work. Make sure it happens!

Playing with your kids ensures that you will also be able to teach your kids. Take charge of those extra seventy-two hours a week, and make them happen for you!

Lord Jesus, help us provide our children with good things to do, good things to experience, good things to enjoy. Thank You that You are the giver of all good things.

Day 43

Greater love has no one than this, that someone lay down his life for his friends." (John 15:13, ESV)

I gave one more swipe of paint and brushed hair out of my face. It was a hot day, and I had decided to tackle the bathroom walls. Outdated wallpaper would surely make the year less pleasant—of that I was certain—so I began ripping away.

A friend had been over and helped me loosen the outer layer. It peeled off nicely, but the glued-on leftovers were a grueling grizzle. I worked an hour, only to see a small part of the wall bare—and that part was jagged up by my putty knife.

Not worth it. At all.

But today as I edged those walls in dark gray over the KILZ I'd previously put on, I was willing to put in hours (and more hours) for the end result. I woke at six and quietly painted away as the kids slept. Two and a half hours later, the walls and trim were edged in a lovely gray.

It took only thirty minutes to push my roller over the mid-walls. But then, there was the trim. It was that nasty, orange wood, and I wanted white. The doors were cheap, old, and had knobs just as ugly.

I began swiping white paint over them after removing the knobs and spraying them with metallic spray paint. The trim got a layer of white as well, after I had spent a while taping the walls off.

But one layer wouldn't cut it; everything needed three layers—and when I pulled the tape off, I needed to touch up where I hadn't taped securely enough. The knobs needed to be put back on, and each towel holder re-screwed into walls.

I was still painting at 5:00 p.m. I worked through heat and chemical smell, determined to have a change of scenery on those old bathroom walls.

And then it hit me. I'm willing to work this hard because it means enough to me.

Something else hit me. No one else will do this for me, and I need to get it done if I want it done.

In fact, no one else will do any of the most important things for me. I must do for myself what no one else can do.

No one else can pursue God for me.

No one else can make me the mother I want to be.

I could have decided not to work at this mess of a bathroom. I could have gone the winter with yucky walls and felt depressed each time I looked at them. I could have sat with a good book and a latte on that hot summer day.

But nothing good comes easy. Mothers and wives, *nothing good comes easy.*

We expect it to come easy and assume we're doing something wrong if it's difficult.

We like to smile when we feel like it.

We even like to mother well when it's convenient for us to do so.

And talking with Jesus as our Friend through this mothering experience doesn't always happen unless we engage our hearts toward Him.

I was willing to work hard for those gray walls enhanced with white trim. Am I going to resent giving other things today, to people who need me even more than that bathroom needed me?

I did the bathroom for myself. Am I willing to give lavishly for others?

The next morning, a tiny voice on the other end of my phone line asked me if she could come over. I said yes, remembering that I am willing to exert effort for everything important to me—and she was important.

Why in the whole wide universe would I be willing to take many hours for a wall when I'm not willing to slow down for a person?

When we're most rushed, we're often most annoyed. We get so bent on that project or chore that the slightest interruption becomes a trial. And in that moment, we choose.

We choose, all over again, many times daily, what is worth our effort.

We say yes to the handicapped person who wants to come over just to hang out with people. We give her a ride, let her stay in our home, then drop her off at home where she lives alone. Our children see what we do, who we love, and how we love.

We cut out some activities so we can carve in Bible time with our kids.

We say no to those brand-new designer clothes for our kids so we can use our money for things more profitable than boosting their ego by wearing too many dollars on their skin.

Because people and their hearts are God's heart—and both they and God know when we give most effort to things while leaving little time for the most important people.

Jesus Himself gave thirty-three years on this planet just for me, for us. He became vulnerable in the form of a man, though He was God—not for an hour, but *thirty-three years.*

If Jesus left heaven to give me thirty-three years on a planet full of sin because He wanted to show me His love, how can I not give a day, an hour, a minute to that person who needs my love—which, in fact, is His own love given me to pass out to His people?

I'll enjoy those bathroom walls and appreciate the beauty of them each day—but may I always hold greater worth and be willing to give even more effort to the things that matter most!

Father, help me willingly sacrifice for the good of my family and all those around me, each and every day.

Day 44

Better a small serving of vegetables with love than a fattened calf with hatred. (Proverbs 15:17, ESV)

The minivan was dusty as usual, and piled high with schoolbooks, a slow cooker of beans, and five kids. I could only claim four, but there seemed to be an extra at hand much of the time. It's good for kids to live life together.

One child is turning eleven on Saturday, and we're headed to Walmart for Oreos and gummy worms. We've already put in a long day at homeschool co-op, but this seems to be the best time to get those promised dirt cake ingredients.

Today, we all look clean and are dressed well. I'm glad, because trudging the aisles with five in tow is often looked on as crazy, done only by overtired women who sigh and moan and wish to be delivered from the mess of kids long before they're grown.

Some days, though I love mothering, I join the crazy mob, wear my ugliest clothes, and pin my hair up in an overly messy bun. Even the kids laugh at me, standing there with a strict tone to my voice and hair all askew.

One day, they will know. Like, really know. *And they will never, ever laugh again!*

I think motherhood is a badge to be worn proudly, even though just this morning I spent thirty minutes on the phone debriefing with my mother. While I did that, all hidden away in the bathroom because that's the only safe place for a mama to hide, the kids were creating more havoc in the dining room where they were supposed to be studiously hovering over books.

How do we successfully navigate those head-knocking days when the kids fight all day and the laundry piles high and we hear the word "mama" two hundred times in twelve hours?

We hear it often, this idea that moms need to escape for "me time." I agree. Times out with friends—or on my own—refresh me greatly. But I think there's more to refreshment than this.

The first thing, for me personally, is to love what I do; to sink into it, to embrace this time fully. Knowing you're exactly where you want to be is the first step to making something work well.

The second thing is to shun laziness and do everything required to make a house a home. Wash those windows, cook that meal, fold that laundry whether your spirits are soaring or not. Living each day faithfully means the years unfold beautifully and your house is truly a home.

We forget the importance of our job when we begin loathing small tasks like scrubbing toilets and packing lunches. What would the world be like if no one did those things? Terrible, right? Which makes our homemaking duties imperative.

The third thing is what I've been getting at. More than escaping our mommy world for a night out, we need to make our mommy world a haven.

You can't truly be refreshed by a night away if the bulk of your life wears you thin. It's a bit like thinking one gasp of air will keep you alive for a whole week.

What wears us down most? Fighting kids? Then let's make it our goal to reduce fighting. If one child wears you out daily, find out what you can do to get him over himself and into being a loving contributor to your household.

If you need wisdom in the area of training your child, find someone who can help you. We owe it to our kids, the world, and God to have the wisdom and training it takes to lead them to peace.

Do chores tire you each day? Perhaps some need to be eliminated. It took me a while to let go of high goals and begin buying more pre-made foods rather than making everything from scratch. When you are in a full season of life, there is no shame in taking some shortcuts.

Because mornings have been full and stressful for me, my kids sometimes make their own bowls of oats. I'm not less of a mama for ignoring the eggs; in fact, my five-year-old thoroughly enjoys pushing chairs around to reach the oat container, pouring his own milk makes him feel like a big boy, and he loves drizzling honey. And lately, it's been cereal—that boxed cereal I didn't grow up on has now become a staple in my own home.

Practical answers can pave the way to spiritual grace in our homes.

What are your stressful moments? What exhausts you most each day? Did you know you are a loved daughter of the King, whose will for you is to be more than a servant worn so thin you can't relate to your status as royalty?

Yes, you may be surrounded by a mess each day, but there are ways to get the mess in your heart under more control than the mess in the house. If we can't do both, let's at least do the most important part!

Father, we need keen insight on how to reduce daily stress. Help us simply refuse to stress out about things happening around us 24/7. There are so many opportunities to stress but You give us an even greater call to peace. Help us cultivate peace in our homes.

DAY 45

For I know the plans I have for you, declares the Lord, plans for welfare and not for evil, to give you a future and a hope. (Jeremiah 29:11, ESV)

Your impossible scenario is God's platform for working His possible solution.

The kingdom of heaven is marked with solutions.

My one dear child is quite strong-willed. Yesterday, I tried something new. Disrespect to Mama means her privileges are taken away for the day. This includes all technology, all classes outside the home, trips to the library, and sometimes even her favorite food.

The next morning, we begin fresh and she gets opportunities based on the respect she shows her mama during that day. This way, she has motivation to change because if she doesn't, her life changes in ways that will be unpleasant to her.

I'm a mercy person and don't always like the hard. This means a strong-willed child won't get the repercussions needed to create change. But, a lesser discipline won't be worth her sacrifice, and if I don't step up, the days will unfold with the same issues causing the same tension in the atmosphere.

The kingdom of heaven is marked with solutions. Though the way is long at times and we don't know how to get there, our hearts can be fully assured that with God, there is peace. As our children get older they need to choose that for themselves—and in seasons where they may not, we can still bring peace into our own atmospheres by relying heavily on grace.

Slow down, end the vicious cycle. Eliminate activities, even good ones, if your family is always on the go, go, go with more stressful moments than are good for anyone. It's up to us to chart a course that makes way for moments in time to unfold, rather than crash, upon us and our families.

Last night, due to all screen time and activities being removed from her life, we found ourselves together, alone, chatting and laughing and sharing hearts. *This never would have happened had I not taken the disrespect seriously and taken action.* She would have continued the rushing about and most likely would have had another day of dishonoring those around her.

Instead, I hear her beyond my bedroom door dancing with the rest of the kids, singing, and making a tea party for her younger sister and friend.

Kingdom solutions make for heavenly moments.

Jesus asks us to pray in this way, "Your will be done on earth as it is in heaven" (Matthew 6:10 ESV).

We all do better giving advice on the sidelines than we do implementing good advice in the thick of things. This is why it's so vital to pause in our mothering rush and take inventory before the months flow into years and we end up wondering how we could have allowed things to slip this long.

Today, take inventory of your life, and dare to make some great, big, sweeping changes! Or, dare to make ones so small you don't see, as of yet, how large the impact will be on your heart. Whatever you do, don't keep pushing, because pushing so hard against a load too heavy will doubtlessly push you right beyond the realm of wholeness and grace.

It is your privilege, even as a mother, to live fully, to walk in wholeness, to breathe grace.

Lord Jesus, thank You that with You everything is full of possibility. There is nothing on this earth that You do not have a solution for. Help us lean into hope and solutions rather than despair and apathy.

Day 46

Have I not commanded you? Be strong and courageous. Do not be frightened, and do not be dismayed, for the Lord your God is with you wherever you go. (Joshua 1:9, ESV)

His teeth sparkled as he grinned wide, right into my face. What a smirk this child had!

I had just dropped off one child for a week of camp. The suitcase packed, along with some snacks and two new dresses for the special dinner they'd be having.

Earlier that day, we'd had some trouble and I'd needed to give her some consequences for disrespect to her mother. We'd been out to pick something up from a friend when the sassing started. I'd whipped the van around and turned back home, headed to her room with her, and sat her on her bed for a pep talk. She hates pep talks. So do I. But sometimes, they need to be given. And because she chose disrespect, I chose to charge her five dollars each for three stressful encounters with her.

She had cried, and I've never been great at handling anything other than peace. So that day, as I pulled away from her favorite summer camp after dropping her off, I blinked back one or two tears. The pep talk was over and she was where she wanted to be, but I hated conflict and didn't like doing what it took to train a strong-willed child.

Life for a mother isn't about herself. It's about a child's good. And we may feel as though we give, and give, and give—and then, all we want is love-filled eyes and sparkling happiness.

That's not life. Real life means you need to say no, it means you love a child earnestly who rather thinks he's ahead of the game and you're behind, it means rather than pass over attitudes, you choose to give your consequences because they chose to give their disrespect.

No matter how it makes you feel.

Mothers, we are full of feeling. But the soul of our child is not dependent on our feelings. If you feel rejected or hurt, rise to the occasion and remind yourself that your child isn't the one who determines your worth, and right now you get to play the adult role by maturely handling the situation.

You get to say "I'm sorry" if you were wrong.

You get to give consequences even if it makes them seem more resentful at the moment (in the long run, it makes them less resentful).

You get to mother up, brave up, love up, and give one more time.

You get to drive them to a friend's house to borrow shoes for the dinner, and then, you get to turn that car around so you can give consequences for disrespect that happened in the car.

You get to nurture them, and then, you get to let go of the same ones you're so attached to.

You get to give them wings, even when you don't know how.

I come home and the six-year-old son teases me as soon as I enter. I look into his eyes, and we rub noses—because that's what we do when Mama's heart needs an outlet for the love bubbling inside as I look into his bright blue eyes.

He even got those long lashes. The girls don't think it's fair—but truth is, they got them, too.

We cuddle up for stories, and he chooses the Bible storybook we read from daily. I ask him, "Son, why did God create you?"

He's teasing me with silly answers, and it hits me as I gaze into his little face. "Buddy, God made you for Himself because He wanted you in His world. He didn't make you for yourself, Buddy. He didn't make you so that you could stand out for your own glory—because really, you're a small part of His great, wide universe and there are lots of people here whom He loves just as much as He loves you."

The life on that little face, the propensity toward himself and his own pursuits apart from God, the charm of his boyhood mixed with the reality that he's one in a million, all created for God, startles me into this God-conscious awareness of the purpose of our existence.

Mothering is hardcore business. We get to give, give, and give some more whether or not we receive anything in return.

We get to live the ups and downs of each child, wear the adult T-shirt each day, and do the right thing no matter how we feel.

Because we, too, have been created by God for His own universe, and our feelings in any given situation are not the deciding factor of what needs to be done.

It's up to us to be *brave*.

Father, thank You that we can be brave as we lean into You. You are strong, always good, and You intend to lead us into that goodness right in the middle of stress and fear. Thank You for providing a way through and filling us with courage. Thank You for making us brave.

DAY 47

Whoever is slow to anger has great understanding, but he who has a hasty temper exalts folly. (Proverbs 14:29, ESV)

I looked at the two little boys, one a husky dark-skinned child who could slay all the dragons in the world and the other a fair-skinned, nerdy child who will most likely be designing computer software someday.

We were spending the summer together in the same house, and the contrasting personalities pushed every single button the other had. One child bossed the other around daily, constantly frustrated that play wasn't unfolding the way he envisioned. The other child pushed back, his fear of rejection causing him to feel left out and unloved.

We mothers nearly pulled out every single hair we owned. Both of us realized that, though there were reasons for the behaviors, they were not excuses.

In real life, bossiness gets you nowhere but to live life alone with no one to boss around. People don't like hanging out with controlling people.

In real life, pushing yourself to the top means you get to tumble all the way down. People don't like bragging.

So, we mothers both kept at it. We knew what they didn't know, that feelings can't always dictate behavior, and that is true *no matter why you feel the things you feel.*

Understanding a child's history can help you identify the cause of behavior, but it must never keep you from consistently training away the behavior.

My son had loved order from the start. He lined his cars and trucks in tidy rows rather than roaring about the floor with them. He drew intricate patterns on paper. He was concerned with cracks in pavement and had certain routines he loved doing each day.

All this was no excuse for him to be controlling, snapping at his little friend when he tried to join in. His personality helped me understand his behavior, but did not explain it away. I needed to lead him to better things.

We spoke with him often, teaching him to invite others into his play. We caught him snapping at others and tried to teach him to ask for what he wanted politely. Many, many times he was sent to his bed or received some other consequence.

I knew that if I didn't help my son, he would grow up with unpleasant tendencies that would create difficulty in his friendships or even his marriage. So while I tried to encourage his gifts, I also required him to let go of perfection.

He may be an engineer someday. His brain works in intricate ways that fascinate the rest of us. But it is up to us parents to encourage the good while training away the bad, and that's true *no matter what the cause of their negative behavior.*

Your strong leader child doesn't need to boss around and criticize everyone daily just because she's gifted with strength. Your mercy child doesn't need to succumb to negative emotions daily just because he's tenderhearted. And your pack of little kids doesn't need to terrorize someone's living room late at night just because they're tired or have had too much sugar. You can train them to go to the van when you're ready to leave, or lay down quietly in your arms when they're too tired.

Our Western culture of nonjudgment and acceptance is creeping into our child training as we give a plausible reason for nearly every bad behavior. Kids are ruling their worlds when they should be guided and kept by wiser adults.

Walk your child through his tendencies, then gently (and firmly, if need be) guide them to acceptable behavior. You must love your child enough to give him the guidance and training he needs. Anything else is not love, but rather laziness and a counterfeit proposal of what love really looks like.

The two little boys learned this summer, and they will keep learning. We mothers won't stop, because if we end the training, their negative tendencies will just lead to more suffering later in life.

Understand your child, then train your child!

Father, help us always understand where our child's actions stem from. Help us lead them to solutions rather than merely deal with symptoms. Help us always lead them to better things.

Day 48

Not that I have already obtained it or have already become perfect, but I press on so that I may lay hold of that for which also I was laid hold of by Christ Jesus. (Philippians 3:12, ESV)

I smiled when milk spilled onto the table and glass shattered everywhere.

Say, whaaaat?!

It didn't take long into mothering for me to decide that I wasn't going to be one of those mothers who got angry when something broke.

My little girl looked at me quickly as liquid gold pooled around the rest of the dishes on the table and dripped through the cracks onto the floor. My eyes met hers in a brief moment as I tried to convey that everything was just fine.

I had adopted a line for my children when they broke dishes. "Everyone makes mistakes."

Children struggle enough with feeling "not OK" and there's enough genuinely bad behavior to train a child through without adding mistakes to the list.

Reproving a child for an accident is nothing short of selfish. You're not helping, training, or protecting your child when you grouch over broken glass and spilled milk.

I want children to see goodness in their mothers. I want us to show them a few things that will stick with them for the entirety of their lives.

It's OK not to be perfect.

I can make mistakes and still be loved.

I'm accepted outside of performance.

I'm human, and Mom is OK with that.

I'm more important than material possessions.

I don't have to earn my mother's love.

It's possible to breathe through stress (I watched my mother do it).

I can tell my mother everything and she'll love me just as much as before.

Life lessons have a huge impact, starting with something as simple as love over spilled milk.

The gift of love you give a child when he makes a mistake may be one of the most important things you will ever do for him. Some may call it acceptance, still others call it security and well-being. Whatever you may call it, this sense of "being OK and safe" is vital to your child as he grows up in a world that offers him many, many alternatives should he face that normal adolescent sense of not being enough.

Drugs offer an exorbitant amount of self-confidence during the high they give. Peers offer group hugs, love, and acceptance no matter what, and that approving slap on the back your child has been craving since his early years.

There's a reason people say of a teen with a troubled home life, "Of course he's doing drugs." It doesn't take rocket science to know that this teen isn't trying to be evil or destroy himself—he's trying to fill a deep void of not being enough or not being OK.

Everyone wants to feel confident, yet many of us face debilitating feelings of not being enough, not being important, and being passed by. I want us mothers to pull our kids away from the world by pulling them toward love and belonging in our homes.

The goodness of God led you to Himself, Mama. His kindness drew your own soul in. Just the same, nothing short of goodness will draw your child. Nothing short of love in all his imperfections will pave the way to God.

I love catching myself in the dreadful moment when I hear a mighty crash, then walk into the room to see milk everywhere, running under furniture and into everyplace milk is not supposed to be. I love watching my child's face tense up with regret, then relax as he looks into my eyes and sees that everything is OK.

I love doing that because I know what it's like to live under constant criticism, and just want to be loved without being perfect. I get to offer that to my child. What a privilege!

Mistakes are not sins, and every adult makes them, too.

Surrender to that moment of spilled milk, and you'll invite heaven into your child's life one small step at a time.

Father, help me instill confidence and a deep sense of well-being into my children even though they are imperfect. Help me lead them through mistakes with love rather than push them through with criticism.

DAY 49

Even a fool who keeps silent is considered wise; when he closes his lips, he is deemed intelligent. (Proverbs 17:28, ESV)

My daughter's voice filled the kitchen as she expressed her thoughts to me that day.

"Can you believe I used to want to tap dance?" she asked. "I was so little and had such silly ideas."

"Yes, I can," I replied. "And I wish you still did. I think it would help you relax and not focus on being strong all the time."

Her countenance fell. "Mom, I was just talking to you, just thinking aloud. Can you please not do this?"

Oh boy. I had done exactly what I didn't like to have done to myself. I jumped on a perceived opportunity for teaching when all she wanted was just to think aloud with her mama in the kitchen.

Allowing a child to just talk is one of the greatest gifts we give them. Not every thought they share has to be balanced in the moment. Life is full of opportunity for you to teach your child, but may not be full of opportunity for your child to talk and *just be*.

Learn to listen, listen, listen. Then empathize. Then, if need be, bring in a teaching moment. But there are many times, even if a need is there, that the teaching moment is not. A better time will come in the future if we practice listening.

"And these words that I command you today shall be on your heart. You shall teach them diligently to your children, and shall talk of them when you sit in your house, and when you walk by the way, and when you lie down, and when you rise" (Deuteronomy 6:6&7, ESV).

We see the mandate from God to lead our children in good paths. We take it to heart as we should. But, have we also listened to his mandate to be quick to hear?

The best teaching moments come *after* the longest times of listening.

Allow grace to govern your listening.

Listen hard.

Listen well.

Remember that not all problems are successfully addressed right in the moment.

Remember that if you wait, a good opportunity for guidance will present itself and it will feel good to take it.

"Why do we feel so uneasy as soon as someone's not happy?" I asked my sister one day. "It's like I think I have to do something immediately to fix it rather than embrace the idea that many times someone will have a gripe or grief or sadness or thought that is not up to me to fix at all."

Sometimes it just is what it is.

Allow your tot to cry without always shushing him right up.

Allow your teen to vent without always preaching at her.

Allow your friends to share problems without having to sound like the wise old owl every single time.

We live in a world of imperfection, yet feel this inner need to perfect each expressed need.

One of the best ways to see growth in our children is by perfecting not them, but our own art of listening well. After we listen well, doors fly open for us to teach well, both verbally and by the subliminal advocacy of our lives.

When it comes to speaking, waiting often brings the wonder of opportunity!

Lord Jesus, help us allow our children to just be, just talk, just express themselves without always taking it as an opportunity to teach when it really is just a moment for expression and friendship. Help us be a safe place just as much as we try to lead them to a safe place.

DAY 50

Remember not the former things, nor consider the things of old. Behold, I am doing a new thing; now it springs forth, do you not perceive it? I will make a way in the wilderness and rivers in the desert. (Isaiah 43:18–19, ESV)

He brought the game and settled on the floor.

Chutes and Ladders, Memory, and puzzles have my six-year-old in stitches of delight, especially when he wins against his mama. With head tilted back, gales of laughter escape his lips as he dramatizes his victory.

The other son nestles his sick head on my lap, and we're all on the floor while rain pours on the roof, whiling the morning away with little things that make for larger love.

Some days, when rain pours and little ones are sick, that's the greatest thing we can do. *Small becomes big.*

Oops! I land on top of the slide, and go all the way down. He giggles with delight, then empathy settles in and he places my person on the wrong block so I can save my spot.

"David, we do what the game rules tell us to do, not what we feel like doing," I tell him. He moves it over obediently.

I reach the top row, wanting to finish this game off and head to other things. But there are many slides on the last row to victory, and down I go again.

Life is a little like Chutes and Ladders. We make one step forward, trying to avoid the slides down. Sometimes, we land on a difficult hill, and down we go. Other times, we hit the ladder and God gives us a mighty upward climb.

After these climbs, there are many opportunities for slides down. Nearing the finish line where we pronounce ourselves winner also means there will be more temptations to slide. But God pulls upward for the win.

Pitfalls do not always mean lack of maturity; rather, knowing how to navigate the pitfalls equals maturity.

Don't be afraid when mothering seems to throw curveballs at you, wanting to get you down. This may be a sign you are near the end of the battle and close to victory. And as in Chutes and Ladders, if you slide down, simply take another step forward toward the finish line.

The day ended, and little boys were prayed over before they trudged upstairs to bed. And I, mama to four precious children, prayed for courage to walk right through those danger zones on to the finish line.

Truth is, one child is visiting relatives out of state, the other child is hiking with a friend, and the third child is having a sleepover with her bestie. I'm washing those dishes feeling a tad bit morose.

Letting go is difficult. I breathe hard, and do it anyway. I don't want to be one of those moms who makes all her choices on what feels good *for her.*

Life is given to the wise rather than the weak.

I lay in bed that night, pondering seasons. A hard season doesn't always equate a wrong season.

We cringe and moan and try to find a way around everything that makes us feel the hard. But rather than try to find a way around it, we must navigate through it. Walking through it means an entirely good world of changes and answers and solutions to each season.

We may also be faced with things we have no answers for. Simply know, in these seasons, that all God wants of you is to do what you know and leave the rest for Him to unfold. He will give you wisdom as He sees you need it; not always as you feel you need it.

Accept what you cannot change—and know this—you will never be perfect enough to change everyone else in your home. Your husband has his own choices to make, and so do your teens. God never asked you to be responsible for their choices; He asked you to listen to His voice for your life.

Embrace what is, and allow God to do a new thing in you whether or not others allow God to work.

We cannot grow from what we avoid. We always grow when we choose to bring solutions into seasons along with courage for the hard.

Your kids don't want to be stagnant. They will grow and change at an alarming rate. Give them wings to fly. The life behind them is changing quickly to the life ahead of them, so focus on preparation and loving the season you're in.

Create life for your kids by embracing the changing life of your kids.

You may feel as if you're sliding constantly, like I did playing Chutes and Ladders with the kids—but remember, you're on a game of growth. Keep spinning the wheel and taking the steps forward with courage even if there are downward spirals at times.

Accept the hard in order to create the beautiful.

Father, help us realize that letting go of our children is the most loving thing to do when they're growing beyond our nest. Thank You for providing security for our hearts as mothers so we don't need to cling to our children staying under our wings. Our security comes from You.

Day 51

Honor everyone. (1 Peter 2:17, ESV)

The word "everyone" refers to all people, including our children. To honor means to prize, to fix value on, to revere.

Especially as our children grow, they need to know their mother values their hearts and cares for their needs.

We show honor by using a firm tone rather than an angry one when they need training.

We show honor by pausing to listen as they speak to us when we're busy and pressed for time.

We show honor as we take time for fun together.

We honor their hearts by feeding them spiritual food in varying ways.

To honor our children is to go out of our way as mothers to ensure all their needs are met.

It's easy to correct or deny what our children are feeling. For example, a child may say, "I'm hungry," right after a meal. We can respond with, "No, you can't be hungry, we just ate." Or we can say, "You are hungry again. But I want you to wait for a little while before you eat again."

If a child is angry or upset, it is easy to reply immediately with, "You shouldn't be angry." We could respond instead with, "This seems very upsetting to you. I can understand why." Then keep listening.

One way shuts your child down; the other allows him to open up, making it easier for him to hear your advice in the end. Hearing your child doesn't mean you accept or condone all his behavior or attitudes—it simply means that you show up for him rather than shut down on him.

There is no better way to walk your child out of his negativity than by entering the difficulty with him. Often, we do the opposite as we stand distant, pushing them toward better behavior. This is counterproductive and not like our Father leads us as adults.

As you acknowledge how upsetting your child's situation must be, he will keep opening up about his problem, during which time you can ask sincere questions to try to understand him.

Do this even if the problem is you. Do it no matter how hard it is. Do it each time.

If you find this impossible, ask yourself why. Why can I not listen when someone has a problem with me? Why do I have the need to perfect each imperfection on the spot, allowing no room for crisis conversations?

He will probably talk his heart out, in the end often drawing a wise solution in his own words. He feels safe to walk through the experience with you at his side because you are in it with him.

In the end, if he doesn't draw a wise conclusion, the door will be wide open for you to guide him to the right answer. He will be ready to listen because he knows you understand.

Another example: A child may say, "My schoolbook is too difficult." We might answer, "No, it's not. Hard work is good for you." The conversation ends, but the child is left feeling like no one understands or cares about his difficulty.

We could say instead, "You are working very hard and I am so proud of you. I would love to help you if you're having a difficult time."

Another example: A child may say, "I hate science!" We may well respond with, "You need to have a good attitude and do things you don't like." Or, we could say, "It's not my favorite, either! But let's keep learning about it so we have some knowledge on something so vital to our world."

Children need to live in an atmosphere of understanding and support where they know their feelings are understood and acknowledged even if we can't always make adjustments for them.

If you have an angry or rebellious child, this could be a huge part of the solution. *Rebellious children often feel alone.*

In his book *Love and Respect in the Family*, Dr. Emerson Eggerichs says:

Empathizing with someone means to share in others' feelings or thoughts, especially when that person is hurt or sad. You try to put yourself in the other person's shoes, and in this case the shoes are worn by your preschooler, your grade school child, or your teenager. You can empathize with your child because you remember what it was like to be new, to be different, to get a poor grade, to lose the game, or whatever it is your child is currently going through.

Lord Jesus, thank You that our children are just as worthy of honor as we are. Help us always hear them and do whatever it takes to make them feel heard. Then, help us be strong enough to make the decision we need to make for their greatest well-being. Thank You that You hear us even when we have difficulty. Thank You for inviting us to come to You no matter how we feel.

Day 52

From the fruit of a man's mouth his stomach is satisfied; he is satisfied by the yield of his lips. Death and life are in the power of the tongue, and those who love it will eat its fruits. (Proverbs 18:20–21, ESV)

My mother had the gift of empathy and made herself my best friend in my teen years. I listened to other girls speak of their mothers and couldn't relate to their disdain and frustration. I realize now that my mother had the ability and desire to relate to me on every level.

We talked, cried, laughed, worked, and shopped together. We shared deepest heart feelings. At times she felt more like a friend than a mother, but she was both.

She walked in empathy and I trusted her.

I say she made herself my best friend because no child can make his mama his best friend. But when we walk faithfully, with love and training combined to create a secure environment for our children, we become more than their mother; we become their friend.

We make ourselves their friend.

My mother had no image to portray, and nothing to lose by saying she was sorry.

A mother who apologizes verbally for her mistakes will find grace and forgiveness from the smallest child up to her teen. Our children see our failures, so for them to see that Mama also knows she messed up and is willing to admit it only grows their respect.

I remember walking with my mama in the woods, and having her turn around to apologize for her earlier frustration to all of us. The scene is seared in one of my earliest memories and has been recalled hundreds of times.

Of course I forgave her.

Saying "I'm sorry" is part of empathy because not only are you acknowledging your own sin, you're saying, "I'm sorry I hurt you, I'm sorry I wronged you, I'm sorry I wasn't a better mother for you."

My mother didn't try to be perfect or sound perfect. She was very human and even snapped at times—because who wouldn't with ten children? But she was humble and loved us beyond herself.

Talk about everything with your children. Start young and never stop. Being a best friend means you are able to address everything life throws at them, from sex to saying "I'm sorry," and everything in between.

Look into their eyes, and just *talk*. Talk especially about things many mothers feel uncomfortable talking about. Talk about them on purpose, often, in a relaxed and free atmosphere where there is no shame. Pull out the goodness of sex in marriage as much as you warn them not to have sex before marriage. Ask them questions and engage each growing season with them.

My own mother is still a safe place. As an adult, I still need her. She hears me and always, always, is glad when I'm happy (and cries with me when I'm not). From a young age until now, she has earned her own place in my world by her extravagant love and extraordinary service to her children.

Lord Jesus, help us look into our children's eyes and talk about anything and everything, from the moment they say their first word until long after they reach adulthood. Thank You for this privilege.

Day 53

For you have need of endurance, so that when you have done the will of God you may receive what is promised. (Hebrews 10:36, ESV)

My son bent over some weeds and mumbled under his breath, "Why do weeds exist, anyway?"

I smiled, remembering my own days of pulling weeds and how my parents equipped me for life by teaching me to push through some back-breaking labor in our large garden. They provided hours of play and happiness. But they never let me slack in helping out even when it was hard.

God Himself allows us the hard in order to learn the good.

Mothers, allow your child to face difficulty. It is good for him to work hard, for there to be times when pleasure is delayed or denied, and to work through friendship issues even when they are painful.

Adult life is full of trials, and a child who learns how to walk through difficulty enters adulthood maturely and well prepared.

I don't hesitate to feed my kids bowls of rice and beans.

I allow them to sweat at pulling weeds.

I read them stories of missionaries who walked through great discomfort to help others.

Children who grow up with the ability to say no to themselves are often those who live life to the fullest. But a child left to raise himself with what he wants is often selfish and difficult as an adult.

Mothers who allow their kids to walk through difficult things and at the same time give their kids fun are the happiest mothers! Those trips to the park with brown bag lunches full of treats, those biking adventures down to the water, those stories read when you are already exhausted, or Friday nights spent sleeping on the floor in one room all add up the happy memories.

The list of possibilities is endless!

Today I watched my three-year-old son scoop potting soil into a flower pot for me. My heart burst at seeing his enjoyment. At that moment, I realized that is how God feels about me when I am blessed. He loves to see my heart full of His peace and joy, loves to pour blessing on me, loves me even more than I love my son.

But sometimes He allows trials in my life in order to grow me into more blessing. He knows I won't be stretched to greater capacity if I'm coddled in my comfort zone.

So our kids, when coddled or rescued at all times, will not grow into resilient adults. Rather than rescue them from all things, we need to help them walk through some tough things.

If their playmate is rude, help them navigate rude behavior. Help them return kindness rather than more rudeness. Help them be strong in the face of meanness. Help them not to always escape, but to navigate. This is best done when you talk about everything from an early age. Create an environment of communication.

And when the weeds are difficult, empathize with them, hand them a drink, but have them finish the job at hand.

In every way, with trials or blessing, may we walk alongside with support and honest encouragement!

Lord Jesus, deliver us mothers from that anxious feeling when our child isn't perfectly happy. Help us walk with them through difficulty, knowing it is a vital part of their development.

Day 54

Jesus said, "Let the little children come to me and do not hinder them, for to such belongs the kingdom of heaven." (Matthew 19:14, ESV)

I remember the week I overbooked my schedule and needed to leave the kids nearly every day. Even though I was occupied with good things, I did not like driving away each day with little hearts missing Mama.

Weeks ago, I had committed to cleaning a vacation cottage twice.

I had joined the worship team at church and we had practice that week, plus I needed to be at church at 7:30 a.m. on Sunday.

I promised to help out with our church's Vacation Bible School, which meant I had a meeting to attend.

A few of my favorite woman friends invited me to go kayaking and I didn't want to miss out.

I planned a breakfast birthday for a dear friend whom I was overdue to celebrate with.

As the week went by, I grew sad each time I left. I missed them and they missed me. My six-year-old began to cry when I left, and I knew there was fighting going on in my absence.

I made money that week and had fun times with my friends, I felt useful at church, and I simply loved worshipping with a group of friends . . . but something was amiss and I was so grateful that life wasn't normally this way.

When possible, we best love on our children when we are home. For me, this looks like taking a job with flexible hours even though another job would be more fun for me. For you, it may look like staying home. For others, it may look like buying dinner so you don't need to cook when you get home from work and can focus your attention on the children. All of our circumstances are different, and God meets us where we are, with what we have.

The time came when my season of singing with the team ended completely *because my children needed me.*

I had to work, but I chose a job that would be less enjoyable but better suited for my children because *they needed me.*

I echo Prophet Nehemiah when he says, "I am doing a great work, so that I cannot come down" (Nehemiah 6:3 NKJV).

There are many things I love to do that I do not allow myself, because I am doing a great work. A great work that can't be accomplished without time and commitment.

If finances are an issue, drive less-expensive cars and be content with a smaller house.

Buy used clothing.

Shop on clearance.

Cook less-expensive food.

Shop at outlet stores.

Most days, make your mocha rather than heading to Starbucks.

Buy off-season clothing in larger sizes to fit your kids next year. (I've walked out of JCPenney with a receipt saying I spent $2.00 and saved $100.) Nowadays, it is entirely possible to dress well but spend very little.

In whatever circumstance we find ourselves, let's be willing to make sacrifices in order to have time with our kids.

Lord Jesus, help us to invite our children to us even when we're busy, just as You did. Help us prioritize our children more than our friends, work, or even ministry.

DAY 55

Do not withhold correction from a child. (Proverbs 23:13 NKJV)

I've seen parents frustrated to the point of desperation as a child yelled and screamed for his own way.

I've seen the helpless look on their faces and heard their voices rise.

I've seen the lack of peace in the child's life as he sasses his way around the world.

He is selfish, mean, *disrespectful*, and unhappy. Parents want only one or two of those little people in their home because that's all they can handle. For good reason! I would be exhausted after an hour.

When you begin not always giving a child what he wants, he will start to understand that the world doesn't revolve around himself.

A two-year-old can understand and be taught to accept a firm "no." He can be taught to sit in his high chair and eat nutritious meals.

A mother does not need to be dishing out snacks every thirty minutes because a child "will not eat." Remove the snacks and after a few days, the child will be hungry enough to eat his meal. He will be satisfied, healthier, and ready to play. After a few hours he will return and you may hand him a nutritious snack to tide him over until dinner, where he will again sit and eat a nutritious meal. *All of this is entirely possible and brings much peace to his life and yours. Of course there can*

164

be circumstances for your child where accommodations and extra grace are given, but this is a general insight my mother taught me in a society where many parents are afraid to train children well.

Children can also be taught to sit in the grocery cart while Mama fills it up. A mother should not need to cease her outings when she has babies (unless she wants to).

The point here is not whether you do the shopping alone or with your children. The point is that, if you want to do it with your children, you can and you should!

Your life is not ruled by the child. Children who fit into their parents' worlds are much happier and well-adjusted than those who call all the shots. Children literally crave a parent's guidance, and their agitation often subsides when they know they are being led.

If your child is accustomed to ruling you, choose one thing and calmly be in control. Sit down and take as long as you need to claim your ground. Stay very calm. Your child will be surprised, perhaps, and try his hardest to win. Stay in charge.

After that, begin a new way of life by leading your child and requiring compliance. Never give up, never give in when he forcefully demands his way. Teach him to ask nicely but still obey if you choose not to give what he wants.

As you learn to be in control, you will feel a new calmness and will notice you are much less prone to raising your voice. Your child may still be resisting, but stick to it, and there will come a day when he recognizes and respects your authority as his mother.

During this time of transition, find enjoyable things to do together and let him know you love him unconditionally. If he is old enough, he will understand your explanation that you have not been following God's way by allowing him to rule you, and from now on you will be in charge because that is how God has set up a family to function best.

He will see your new calmness and begin to feel the difference in his own heart. He will love you more, respect you more. You will be friends, companions with the ability to enjoy life together.

Best of all, there will be a growing appreciation of God and His ways in your young child's life. He will not be confused by a difference in the chaos he feels in the home and the peace he sees elsewhere.

Allowing a child to rule a home means we invite chaos into our home. What we set out to do for a measure of peace ends up disrupting all peace.

Likewise, when we refuse to "keep peace" by handing that child whatever he demands, we actually pave the way to real peace in our homes.

Be strong, and be kind!

Father, help us know that each effort we put into training will reward us in a more peaceful home. Give us vision and grace to do the hard thing so we can all enjoy a peaceful home.

Day 56

Behold, children are a heritage from the Lord, the fruit of the womb a reward. Like arrows in the hand of a warrior are the children of one's youth. Blessed is the man who fills his quiver with them! He shall not be put to shame when he speaks with his enemies in the gate. (Psalm 127:3–5, ESV)

Six kids sat in a row on stage as their daddy preached. They were being interviewed by their daddy on home and church life, giving unscripted answers in front of hundreds of people.

I was impressed. First of all, by the father, who allowed his kids to answer honestly without fear of embarrassment. Secondly, by the fact that all six kids were happy and in love with the same Jesus their parents were.

This does not just happen. What does this family have?

Daddy is a leader who requires obedience. From the kids' own mouths, "There are consequences." They spoke shamelessly of discipline, even smiling while they attested that Daddy is the hammer and Mama is the pillow.

These kids don't live an easy life. Each Sunday, the family attends two services. They serve a whole lot. Daddy comes home in the afternoon exhausted. But he also spends days with his kids on mission trips and vacations. He allows his kids freedom to do enjoyable things without his presence.

He is strict without being restrictive.

Many parents are both strict and restrictive. They parent out of fear and allow almost no liberties for the child. Other parents hold firm guidelines but grant an open place for their child to experience life, fun, and people.

When a child has both, the dynamics are powerful.

These six kids also had a dedicated mama. She honored her husband well. Everyone knew her heart was behind him and she supported him in any way she could. She spoke to us ladies with her adopted daughter in a carrier on her back and was graced with a quiet strength all of us could feel.

This lady could speak in front of hundreds of people, or sit quietly on the front chairs for two services in a row. She could travel to important meetings or cook breakfast for twenty families who came in for retreat. In all of it, she carried a grace and poise about her. She was never loud, didn't demand attention. She just was. She knew her calling and fulfilled it well. But we could all tell it flowed from a heart convinced that *God knew her name and had called her to her task.*

The oldest daughter went off to college with simple grace and beauty. She was like her mother, quietly confident. The second daughter was the same, and the third child, a son, surprised all of us by breaking his normal quiet as he spoke into the microphone with passion. A sixteen-year-old son with that much energy for the Lord was both astounding and refreshing.

The fourth child was a bright-faced daughter who was known for her smile. Countless times I saw her give up her own desires for something else, without creating drama.

And the fifth and sixth children were normal little tykes with happy faces who gave answers that made us erupt in laughter. The youngest loved church because of the nursery, her favorite thing was a bakery, and as is typical of four-year-olds, it was all about her.

I learned about mothering from watching this family, learned how to require sacrifice from my children while also giving them opportunity.

Give them freedom in proportion to their character at home.

Teach them that at-home behavior is a gauge of what they are ready for outside the home. Countless times, this has given great incentive to kids to overcome character needs they seemingly couldn't get over.

Expect your child to make mistakes and display dire character needs. This is part of being human, of growing up. Expecting it releases you from frustration when an immature moment occurs once again. *The key is to lead them to something better, something higher than themselves.*

If kids learn that life is not all about themselves, they have come a long way. A child who learns that everyone is important is much less prone to pout when someone else gets his own way. She will work with the group instead of in her own world, for herself.

I'm thankful for examples like this family as I mother my own children!

Lord Jesus, assure our hearts that giving to our children does not look like giving them everything they want, but being wise with what they need. Give us wisdom beyond our own to know what that looks like for each child.

Day 57

Children, obey your parents in everything, for this pleases the Lord.
(Colossians 3:20, ESV)

"Hey kids, it's time to leave!" a mother yells.

Ten minutes later she calls the same words.

Ten minutes later, she climbs the stairs to drag little Johnny unwillingly out the door while she shoots apologetic eyes at the hostess and plops the child in his car seat.

This sounds familiar to a lot of mothers, but there's a better way to live.

A mama shouldn't need to wait ten minutes while a child decides whether or not he will crawl into the car when it's time to leave. She should not need to bait him with promises of a treat to get him to obey. A simple request should always be met with prompt obedience.

This should become your norm, not your surprise.

Mothers who train this way experience a rest and joy in mothering that astounds other mothers. For no small reason! How much easier is it to say, "Son, it's time to leave," and have him walk over and get in the car without fuss? Rather than ten minutes of coaxing and waiting while you hope your friend doesn't become weary of your chaotic presence.

How much easier is it to cook a meal and serve it to a hungry, thankful child than to have him refuse your hard work, then beg for snacks (his choice) all afternoon?

How much easier is it to say no to a child at the grocery store and have him wait quietly than to carry a screaming child out to the car?

But how, you may ask, do I get there?

The law of sowing and reaping applies to all human beings, including our children.

Emily's son had a dog and wasn't caring for him responsibly. Emily grew weary of repeated reminders and told him they would get rid of the dog unless he showed responsible care in the next week. He did.

Mary's daughter couldn't stand her younger sister. Mary felt like she lived in a war zone each day, and dreaded waking up the girls because without fail, a fight would ensue. She was not naturally as strong as her friend Emily. Ironically, as Mary told her child of Emily's method of discipline, Mary's daughter said, "Mama, you should give us strong disciplines like that. It would work so much better."

All we can say to comments like that is, sometimes children know what they need better than we do!

Stacey's son refused to eat his meals. She grew weary of continual snack messes and decided to remove them until he ate nutritious meals. He was willing to put up with a few hours of hunger, after which he decided to eat his dinner. A few hours of discomfort gave her years of peace, and him a lifetime of wiser food choices.

It may take days or weeks for a stubborn child. Don't give up or give in. Children are not wise enough or experienced enough to know what they need.

We are, but sometimes we are not strong enough to follow through or too lazy to do the work it takes to guide them into wise behavior.

Sometimes kids are smarter than we are. Actually, a lot of times. And often they know what they need even when they are fighting the process. This is why they need us to do it for them.

Mamas, we don't get to be immature. The soul of our child is depending on us.

Lord Jesus, show us that our choices have far-reaching effects and our feelings have little to do with determining what we should do with and for our children. Give us vision with clarity and strength for what needs to happen in our homes.

Day 58

For I have chosen him, that he may command his children and his household after him to keep the way of the Lord by doing righteousness and justice, so that the Lord may bring to Abraham what he has promised him. (Genesis 18:19, ESV)

"Yellow bear, yellow bear, brown bear, Yellow bear, yellow bear . . ."

"Which one comes next, David?" I asked my four-year-old son.

He knew brown bear was next in line, but because he liked yellow bear more, he chose yellow bear. I took the opportunity to help him lay down his desires for the right choice.

"They want brown bear, David. That's what comes next." So he circled brown bear.

Everyday matters can help us guide our children to make the right choice even when they don't feel it. This can start very young.

Most good things in life require hard work. A child doesn't grasp that fact, but at a very young, tender age we can (and must) begin shaping them toward the right *whether it feels good or not.*

I love having fun, engaging, happy, feel-good moments with my kids. I love enjoying life with them and getting in their zone of fun. But sometimes, I also love taking them out of their feel-good zone into what will help them mold character and an ability to choose rightly when something else feels better.

Such as Monday morning. I go upstairs to four sleepy kids who want nothing to do with school at that moment. But, I'm happy to wake them because I know what they don't know—that if they don't learn to get up, prepare for their duties, and do them regardless of whether or not they "feel" like it, their lives as adults will most likely be far less productive, and maybe even be destructive.

It's up to Mama to wake them when they grumble. It's up to me to see ahead to what they cannot see. It's up to me to lead, to grow them into more than they would grow into themselves.

It's up to Mama to take charge of that one-year-old's taste buds by serving her nutritious food.

It's up to Mama to create a healthy interest in productive things by reading good books to her kids.

It's up to Mama to disengage a growing passion for the sensual and evil by refusing to bring certain things into the lives of her children.

It's up to us to say "no" to that child who wants to hang in an unhealthy environment.

It's up to us to have wisdom our kids do not yet have. To be willing to step in and make decisions that will make them less than happy in the present while preparing them for a better future.

We see the greater picture. We see the future, because they need us to.

We're willing to engage in activities when it's easier not to. We're willing to drive farther to meet a good friend than send him off on foot to hang with someone of ill influence.

We're willing to spend money and take time to help them pursue their passions and interests. That daughter who is a tad bit restless but has always had a passion for dancing—maybe it's time to enroll her in classes each week and spend less on something else.

We're willing to sell that car so we can buy a guitar for the son who is growing up and needs useful interests before he's idle enough to get in trouble.

We engage, we pursue, we help them become. We shop less for ourselves and more for them, if that's what it takes to give them all they need for joy-filled, productive lives.

Children are at our mercy. They get what we give.

If the parent has wisdom, he can gift his child by imparting wisdom children have yet to discover—and may never discover on their own.

Jesus, thank You for choosing us to be part of drawing generations after You. Thank You that You've called us to far greater things than ease and materialism. Thank You for purpose far exceeding our own small desires and ease. And thank You for giving us all the strength needed for our task. We love You, Jesus.

Day 59

For I give you good precepts; do not forsake my teaching. (Proverbs 4:2, ESV)

This one really gets me.

On *American Idol*, very young children perform on stage while parents choke back proud tears of emotion. In Amish country, most girls grow up to become competent mothers, cooks, landscapers, teachers. They do the domestic more than well. In California, many girls grow up with great fashion style and spend much time on beauty. They look amazing. The Indigenous people in Ecuador raise boys who can creep through brush-laden forests with no sound.

Children who are exposed to books of lesser content begin craving those very books. Kids who grow up mostly performing become performers, while kids who are taught to love and serve will very likely become empathetic, caring adults.

Children who are corrected and scolded over every little mishap become critical and expect a standard of perfection in others. Children who are praised for perfection often begin to show a "better-than-you" type of attitude, while kids who are loved in their messiness show a much greater ability to relax and encourage others.

When they are loved well, they often love well.

In so many ways, children's homes and parents shape who they will become.

This is not to say a parent who made good choices won't have children who struggle, or even have a wayward child. Some of the best mothers have a child who strays from all he's been taught. But it's up to us to hold the best for them to choose from.

We can hold the best out to them even in the worst moments of struggle with them. Leading our children means walking beside them through some very difficult places as they learn to walk with Jesus on their own.

Parenting means pulling purpose out of low times so we can pull them back to good times. It never means perfection. It never means avoiding excruciating trials. It simply means always being there with the good held out to them with deepest love.

It's time to take inventory of our lives and rediscover some things parents would do well to impart to their children. It's time to be brave enough for change. To realize that the personal becomes far reaching as soon as you wear the badge of parenthood.

Mothers, let's take courage to raise children in ways that our culture does not understand. Let's do it proudly and with grace! Then, let's humbly trust God when we take a child's hand and walk through rougher places than we expected.

There, we learn of the grace of God in ways we've only heard of before. A mother who can walk a child through rebellion or times of testing with the same love as before, is a mother God hears. Her prayers are not in vain and she is not alone.

God is so near to all of us.

Father, You are good. Help us walk our children through hard things while leading them on to goodness. Help us not look for perfection without trial, but look for Your perfect love in the midst of trials.

Day 60

Mercy and truth are met together; righteousness and peace have kissed each other. (Psalm 85:10)

Bam! The small container of Cheerios crashed to the floor and little loops rolled merrily under the table.

She scowled, this tiny, cute little girl, and her mama sighed wearily. It had been a full weekend and here we were, all circled round the table with coffee to savor and thoughts to share.

We are family.

My brother-in-law pulled his mad little cherub onto his lap, and I, a mother of four with eagerness to learn, scooted closer to hear their discourse over angrily spilled Cheerios. I was more than impressed.

He holds her while he asks, "Honey, why did you spill the Cheerios?" And she answers honestly, "I wanted fruit snacks."

Daddy makes her think. "Is it nice to spill Cheerios on purpose?"

The tiny tot shakes her head. She's not squirming, pulling away, or fighting her daddy.

I see here that Daddy has a solid, ongoing, communicative relationship with his daughter that brings her into comfortable interaction even over spilled Cheerios. She feels safe because there is no anger, no tension; only an engaged father willing to ignore the rest of us for a while to get to his daughter's heart.

Daddy continued, "I want you to go pick up those Cheerios."

She did, without a fuss, and soon the entire container was filled by a quiet little girl moving sweetly across the floor. As she trotted away happily, I pondered. Would some parents swiftly remove the child to render a more-severe-than-needed discipline?

How many parents would feel embarrassed and react under pressure?

And how many parents have that type of influence and control over a child's spirit, where they can walk them through their own small crisis, then require a change that is met with prompt obedience?

How many of us can discern when a child needs to talk and when he needs a consequence? We sometimes give consequences for actions when a loving talk would get to the child's heart even better. We forget that God uses many, many means of getting our attention, and more times than we deserve, He uses patience over the course of years to teach us one thing.

The child who fights over everything may not respond like this child did, and therefore may need greater consequences. Sometimes, we're blessed with kids who seem to learn only the hard way. Faithfulness requires us to follow through because when we don't, our homes are in chaos.

But kids obey more easily when they are also drenched in loving interaction, when Mother talks with them, when there are no raised voices or consequences given in anger.

We must always, always, speak kindly. If necessary, we may walk away for a moment to get our own emotions under control before engaging our child.

Explain why their actions were wrong, what you expect them to do, and then, follow through. If the child easily complies like the angry little birdie who whacked Cheerios out of her mama's hands, your job is easy. If she doesn't, your duty to her, your family, the world, and God, is to persevere and not to give in to the child's disobedience.

Time spent with an unyielding child is well spent. You must not, cannot, leave the situation until she is well aware that Mama calls the shots—not her.

Failure to follow through invites chaos to your home. Time spent leading your child to submission means opening your doors to peace, grace, and love. Make sure you learn how to love well, and then, ensure you are leading well.

We can't afford to do just one or the other. In each and every situation with our child, we must have both kindness and authority. Only kindness leads to chaos; only authority leads to rebellion. Your child needs both.

Father, help us to meet each incident with our child with as much mercy as truth and as much truth as mercy. May they see, through us, that love and truth go hand in hand and can never be separated.

Day 61

May the God of hope fill you with all joy and peace in believing, so that by the power of the Holy Spirit you may abound in hope. (Romans 15:13, ESV)

I was the mother sitting in the pastor's office talking about hope— because I needed hope, and I'd been scrambling for it a bit like my son scrambled for fireworks on July 4th.

We'd been at a large pool party on the lake and he had already enjoyed more than our usual celebrations there. But there's nothing like fireworks for a little boy.

I contemplated running out to buy some, but prayed instead.

A pop here and there throughout our neighborhood pierced the air, and we'd drop what we were doing and run toward the sound only to see a vapor of smoke disappear. This went on for a while until we burst out laughing over our silly sprints from one end of the yard to another.

But the longing was there. My little boy needed fireworks in his new neighborhood. And being new to town made me unaware of where the crowds met to view them.

I took his hand and walked down the road toward the louder noise piercing the night air. As darkness settled in we sat on the grass and watched as the sky lit up brighter than we'd ever seen before, and the air became heavy with smoke.

I laid on the grass and looked up. It was beautiful. Could I see hope in the same way?

The pastor mentioned previously looked at me a few weeks later with his eyes all lit up with hope, and I wished to reach right in and take hope, experience hope, feel hope for myself. I knew what he said was true—*there were good things coming*—but I was still dreading the future.

But hadn't Jesus made promises to me that I could convey to my children? In this time of loss and what should have been financial hardship, we had plenty. On the Fourth, my little boy had an ice cream truck full of treats, a lake to swim in, and an in-ground pool to enjoy along with catered food, all free of charge from the generous hospitality of friends.

God had been stepping up for my children and me in ways that blew me away. But I was still fighting despair.

I took my son's hand and walked toward the house. "I prayed for those fireworks," I told him.

And a few weeks later as he's drenching himself under a waterfall in the heart of the Blue Ridge Mountains, he says, "I can't believe God made this for us!"

Mothers, our privilege and duty is to bring hope to our children in a hopeless world. We do that when we see God. We do that when we point out the works of God. We do that when we lean into God when our world is falling apart by circumstances beyond our control.

Children need hope. They don't need to see you hopeful because your life is coming together as much as they need to see you hoping in a God who holds the universe together.

Point out all the works of God. Notice them, count them, list them, enjoy them. Training our children in gratefulness can only happen when we are taken with appreciation.

Abundant life begins with gratefulness. Pure, raw joy starts with appreciating the gifts before you each day.

This, mothers, is why you will see one person full of joy even in trials, and another person with a relatively easy life griping and complaining. *Hope is not contingent on your circumstance looking hopeful, but on allowing the God of hope to come into your circumstance and permeate it with His gifts.*

The God of goodness still rules the world and He calls us to delight in goodness.

I walked out of the pastor's office with a smile lighting my face. I knew his words were true. The God of hope was with me, in me, for me—and there were good things coming even when I didn't know what they were.

I could keep giving the gift of hope to my children. Mothers in hard places, so can you—and together we can all show our children what it means to lean into a God of hope when we need it most.

Father, You are the Father of mercy and the God of all comfort. You embody hope. Help me show that to my children and lead them, always, to see Your goodness in this world.

Day 62

What then shall we say to these things? If God is for us, who can be against us? (Romans 8:31, ESV)

Staci looked at me and cried.

"I hate this!" she sobbed. "I don't want to be treated like this any longer."

She had just been in a difficult conversation with her child, and the heat had been delivered. And she wondered, as many of us mothers sometimes do, why was there so little respect shown her when she had given so much?

I listened to her cry, and I shed tears with her. Then, we talked about not allowing others to control our emotional well-being.

Staci had never learned that she was a free agent. She'd based her own soul's well-being on what was delivered her by other humans rather than on what was freely given her by God. This kept her captive to what went on around her, and consequently (because people are messy), her inner world was shattered.

She'd entered the older years and was wondering if there was hope for a more peaceful existence. Like Sara of old, who doubted that God's promise of a child could materialize because of her age, Staci doubted that life would afford her the blessings she longed for because she had grown older and her child was still disrespecting her.

She gripped her cup of tea and looked at me brokenly.

Some of us look at wrong behavior and rise up to correct it. Others of us feel the effects of disrespect so greatly we fall down under it.

Then, we learn the word *boundaries*. Like a child peering through a darkened doorway, we listen warily.

We hear about not reacting to another's actions outwardly, but redeeming them internally.

We hear about not waiting for someone to do something for us, but getting it done for ourselves.

We read about saying *no* when another tries to control us. Because another's attempt to control us is not what's controlling us—*it's our yes to their attempt that brings us under their demands.*

See this—no one can control you. Just as no one can walk into your house and demand you allow them to live there, so no one can force you to do anything.

When someone tries to control you, you must learn not to react, but to respond with a loving, firm *no*. If you've been one of those sweet, but perhaps resentful people bending over backward for everyone around you like Staci was, you will have to learn the blessed art of saying *no*.

You will cause a ripple. Those around you will label you selfish and have their own attitude to work through, but that's OK. If you create boundaries and refuse to accept disrespect, you will win more respect and love in the end.

Emotional distance is often caused by lack of boundaries and strength on *your own part more than on the part of your child.*

Many times, as in Staci's situation, no one will stand for you. You must learn what tears you up and you must learn to stand up. You can, and you will. But it must be done in firm, loving response rather than angry, reactionary methods.

If your child rudely demands you to get something, stay where you are and ask them to please ask you kindly. If you comply with rudeness, you will be overtaken by it because you are giving yourself to it.

If someone speaks to you in a crushing manner, refuse to react or absorb it. You, and only you, have the power of freedom over your own heart. No one can make you feel low. No one can steal your confidence.

No one can rob you of your promise or hope, even in your old age.

See this—no one can steal from you what God has already given to you. And feeling like you have to escape someone or something can be the driving force to allow you to finally escape yourself.

You are not defined by what you receive from another. You are never forced to feel or do.

You can raise your standards without raising your voice.

You can control yourself while releasing control of those around you.

You can be at peace even if another refuses to grant you peace.

You can wage war while remaining entirely still.

You can create boundaries without creating selfishness.

The things that may cause ripples in another who doesn't like the boundary will be agents for change. Getting up from your doormat requires you to muster strength to stand when lying down is more comfortable.

As St. Augustine says, "The cause, not the suffering, makes a genuine martyr."

Father, thank You that no human on this earth, not even our own children, can rob us of Your peace. What You give is far more powerful than what any human can give.

Day 63

There is no fear in love, but perfect love casts out fear. (1 John 4:18, ESV)

I glanced in my rearview mirror at the four.

They were fighting—already, before the wheels ever rolled.

If anything wears on me, it's bickering. I hate conflict. I'm with the kids all day long and sometimes I want the T-shirt that says, "I Can't Adult Today."

I glance at them again. One is cuddled up in her pink robe, wearing a pink ribbon in her hair, surrounded with pillows and comfort. She'd be happiest handing out kisses and chocolate to people for the rest of her life.

The other is sitting tall, reading with an analytical mind, soaking up the story. "Mama," she says mournfully, "This story is soooooo emotional. They're falling in love and dying of cancer and it's just so sad."

One child is munching snacks for miles, and the other is asking for the hundredth time, "Are we there yet?" And then, they all go crazy and sing silly songs while we fly through sagebrush and wild land.

My mind flies along, too, as I drive, and I treasure these days with the kids all in the car at the same time because one day, they won't be.

We pull into a gas station and they mill about for the promised snacks. *Being their mama makes me question everything.* Am I better for allowing them ice cream and Frappuccinos while we drive, or worse for not having them eat pure nutrition even on the road?

And at home, do I have them eat oatmeal and green smoothies for their vitamin intake, or give them boxed cereal and bottled vitamins? Am I fun enough? Am I too fun?

Some questions are easily answered, and others remain a mystery to solve as the years unfold. I wish they stayed small until I had it all figured out, but they're growing like weeds, and the twelve-year-old is nearly as tall as her mama.

I'm still learning about discipline. I'm still learning about staying calm rather than wanting to lose it when they start bickering *again*.

I keep saying, "Stop fighting or you won't get ice cream."

They keep arguing, and I keep giving consequences. I remember what my mother says, "Just don't let it go unchecked." I breathe a sigh of relief that I don't have to drown in daily conflict—at the least, I can swim, and perhaps I can even swim out of it.

If one child creates a nasty atmosphere and won't stop, buying ice cream for three of them rather than four of them can be as difficult for me as for the child. But if I talk, talk, talk without some consequence to back up my words, things won't change.

Our sweet little children know how to push the lines while we scratch our heads wondering where the heathen attitudes come from. If Mama doesn't put a line up for them to push, they walk right over it into a lifestyle of selfishness and chaos.

I swallow hard and buy ice cream for three children. The fourth child is sober for a while as the message sinks into his head while his siblings sink their teeth into cold creamy heaven.

It's painful to watch.

Mamas don't get to wear T-shirts that say, "I Can't Adult Today."

Mamas need to learn to be adults, because no one grows into a healthy adult if Mama isn't one first.

I drive through the sagebrush with my four, and my heart is alive. Solutions mark the kingdom, and they can mark our parenting, too. *We may never get it perfect, but if that child rests his head on your shoulder and there's that love bond between you two, you don't have to get it perfect.*

Christ comes through for you and woos your child just as He woos your own heart. **The soul of your child is fertilized by you, but planted by Christ.** He has you be the vine keeper, but He owns the vineyard. It remains, then, that staying rooted in Christ and alive in Him is the most important thing to do for your child.

It's all in a day. At the end of the day, our shortcomings are swallowed up in love, and *love wins.*

Father, at the end of each day help us not fret about the lack of perfection in that day, but be taken up and at peace with the abundance of Your perfect and enduring love for each and every day.

Day 64

Casting all your anxieties on him, because he cares for you. (1 Peter 5:7, ESV)

"Mama!" The littlest son dashed into the kitchen. "The toilet!" My heart sank. Sure enough, "stuff" and water that wouldn't flush down and away. I left the schoolbooks and took the weapon in hand, but no amount of plunging would do the trick.

The landlady and maintenance man came over, that guy who always has too many toilets to unclog and too many dishwashers to fix. I feel like a heel, another number on his already-too-long list. He treks back and forth through the kitchen while the landlady sits, and I try to bring some semblance of order to the school table.

A car pulls in, and it's the lovely grandmother who helps me each Friday. She listens to the kids quote Bible verses and gives them spelling words. She's a gem, a real, true gem, our "grandmother" without even trying to be.

Another car pulls in, and it's the friend whose two little ones I had invited over to play. The toilet is still out of commission, and the fixer guy has it tipped while he hoses it down, right on the porch.

He's been batching it out for too long, I suppose, and has forgotten all about germs. The germ-freak daughter who wants to be a nurse someday steps gingerly around the mess trying to hold it in graciously.

The kids run and play dress-up, shoot play guns, and water is dripped all over the kitchen floor from the plumber while the kids run wild. I'm just in the center of the whirlwind, wondering what is most important and where I should be.

I listen to the saintly grandmother seated beside me and I know she's right when she says, "Some things we just can't fix. They are what they are."

Mothers, part of our health depends on allowing other, more-seasoned mothers to speak into our lives. Not just speak, but *walk right into our lives, our mess, our routine—and tell us how to handle it all better than we are.*

She picks up my laundry and folds it. I cringe. Who would want to fold *that*? She never blinks an eye, and all is so soft and tender about her that I know, and we all know, everything's OK even when the toilet's tipped and germ-filled water sinks into the porch floor and runs into the cat dish.

It is what it is.

And we as mothers may creak and groan and try our best to change the chaos into order, when all God wants to do is change the chaos of our hearts into peace.

I feel peace enter my soul as I watch my older friend fold my laundry, as I hear her soothing words, as I humble myself so I can position my life for grace. This is one of the best things I can do for my children.

I need to reach out so I can let others in. I need to speak out my need so my need can be met. My children need me to do this so their own needs can be met, because I can't give what I don't have, and I don't have it all. I was never expected to have it all, and neither were you. ***Allow those mothers in.***

The mess is.

The dirty kitchen is.

The lack of extra time just is.

And sometimes, there are much greater trials going on in your life at the same time, and it just is what it is regardless of how much you wish it wasn't so. Accepting what you can't change and choosing to engage the difficulty of those things with other adults is even more vital than hearing their wisdom for minor things like a messy mothering day.

Allow those saintly people into your life for everything you don't know how to deal with on your own. Let them in. Face your trial head-on as you deal with reality. This is the only way to come to the other side with soul growth and healing.

We'd like to run, hit denial, avoid, or collapse. None of those are good options, but to face reality, you need to let others in who will help you when it just is what it is. Be vulnerable so another's strength can become your own.

The mature, seasoned grandmother hears my heart well so it all comes spilling out, and like leaves softly wafting down through fall air, her words fall on my young mother's heart.

Perhaps more than trying to perfect the days and years, we need to still our hearts and love big, while allowing ourselves to be loved by those who truly know how to love well. Light a candle, smile, look into the eyes of our children because we've seen the eyes of a loving Father on us in spite of those things that are so painful we can't always mention them to our children.

Because despite things being what they are, love is what it is, too. And if we can't have it in those less-than-perfect days and seasons, what do we really have? Isn't love greater than anything?

Love is what it is, and when you have it, you do what it does. You are what it is.

Let life roll crazily, madly, all around you while it never stops for you to catch your breath; but you, mother and friend, you pause in the middle of the swirl, catch that tired breath of yours, and then, *love big*.

If the mess is big, let your love be bigger. If time is scarce, make sure your love is not.

Let the mess be what is, while you do what love does.

Because love-drenched moments are of greater worth than all the time in the world without love. If you have love, then you are love, and if you're love, you saturate those surroundings with something greater than the mess, or the busyness, or the lack of time.

We are conduits of grace. The day is what it is, and life is what it is, but love also is what it is—and love wins every time.

Lord Jesus, thank You for seasoned mothers who can help us younger ones mother better and be OK with life as it is. This season will pass, but Your love is steady through all of life, and You want us to bring it with us as we walk each step with our children. Help us to engage our grief so we can encounter Your grace. Thank You for this privilege.

Day 65

Whoever covers an offense seeks love, but he who repeats a matter separates close friends. (Proverbs 17:9, ESV)

I had baked four pies, and they rested in near perfection on the counter.

Then, I reentered the kitchen to find three little fingerprints on top of the nearest golden pumpkin pie. Four pairs of eyes crowded round, and four little mouths declared innocence.

But the prints were just too obvious. I was confident that my older kids wouldn't lie about something so trivial, so I knelt before the five-year-old and began my motherly speech on truth telling and lies.

Suddenly I felt a tap on my shoulder, and a quiet voice said, "Mom, it was me."

I looked up into large blue eyes brimming with tears.

He was in utter repentance for lying and all he needed was to be held, forgiven, and encouraged to ask God's forgiveness for lying to his mother. I wrapped him in my arms and gave him all the love I could.

Our kids and us are a bit like Christ and us. God often grants undeserved mercy and is always ready to hear us. We adults get to talk with Jesus even when we're not "performing" like we think He would want to see.

What a comfort and joy my relationship with Christ is to me! Just the initial welcoming into His presence regardless of how I'm doing is what it takes to bring me on to something better, right into His heart. We are changed by being held. Christ does have righteousness for us to live by, but we gain access to that righteousness by being close to His heart. We can only live righteously by knowing His heart.

Our kids, when they are young and frustrated, gain even more maturity when they are first listened to before we decide whether or not a consequence is needed. Sometimes consequences aren't needed at all, even though they did wrong. Sometimes all they need is a good heart-to-heart time with a parent who loves them. Other times they do need something to get their attention.

If my son was a habitual liar I would need to implement something more.

God wouldn't be God if He wasn't righteous. He wouldn't be trustworthy if He passed over sin and didn't care. But as with God, we can show mercy and grace when nothing more is needed to guide a child to the right path.

Mothers, use things like a "ruined" pumpkin pie to show your child that you love him more than you love your perfect projects!

Father, thank You for those sweet times of forgiveness when it is both asked for, and granted. Help us to love mercy even if our efforts have suffered from a child's mischief.

DAY 66

I have been crucified with Christ and I no longer live, but Christ lives in me. The life I now live in the body, I live by faith in the Son of God, who loved me and gave himself for me. (Galatians 2:20, ESV)

The third child yelled, and I jolted at the sound of conflict in the other room.

It was only 8:30 in the morning, and I swiped my eye makeup on hastily and rushed out the bathroom door to dissolve the tenth fight of the morning.

Two kids looked at me, each with his own story.

"She's lying."

"No, he's lying."

So began the day. I listened to their complaints for a short while, then gave the verdict, which seemed most appropriately fair. But, as usual, one child was unhappy and utterly convinced that I was incorrect in my judgment.

I walked away, defeated. All that effort would seem worth it if I could leave with both kids aligned in heart and soul, peacefully. I hated the blame I felt. Did I rush them? *Was* I fair? But who could stand there for ten minutes just to listen to them gripe about each other?

Perhaps instead of rushing around making my bed, sweeping a boatload of dirt off the floor, and trying to look presentable, I could be nurturing them a bit more. *I could calm down, quiet down, shut out my own adult world for a while in exchange for theirs.*

I could be present.

Why do kids swarm around with anyone who takes time to talk, really talk, with them? When any one of my friends come over, looks at their small faces, and just talks about all they do and love, I stand back and observe how alive they are.

They chatter. They smile. They love it. They end up thinking my friend is the most amazing lady they've ever met.

I love it, too. To see them alive is my greatest desire.

I take lessons. A mother is never done learning, ever. Today, I learn more about myself, more about them. To walk beside them, to say yes to that son when he asks for a bike ride with Mama, to say yes to the daughter who asks me to listen to her new favorite song, to sit down with the four-year-old and do school with him when I would rather run about doing my own thing.

But even more than doing, there is being.

We can do a lot of things with our kids while our minds are entirely elsewhere, wrapped up in our own adult world. We have a lot to ponder, to question, to walk through ourselves. That's life. But we end up mindlessly teaching math and wiping messes and answering questions and, and, and . . .

I see the frustration in my son's eyes as he wants my focus completely on him. And I resolve to be present, to live life with them as I live it in my dreams. To have a present mind and energy to nurture, engage, and thrive with these little people I spend my days with. No sacrifice is too big (or too small) for these children God gave me for a short while.

Mothers are never *done*.

I remember the morning where my little four-year-old son was so well cared for (I thought).

He woke up earlier than I, asked for a snack, and ate nutritious protein bars. Then I fed him a green smoothie and poached eggs, followed by brushing his teeth with natural tooth powder a friend had given me.

I washed his face and dressed him in his new shirt, then sat down to teach him letters and numbers while I enjoyed a homemade mocha. He looked adorable and I felt warm with the pleasure of caring for my little son.

But then I noticed eggs *behind* his ears. It looked gross and like some mama had forgotten to wash her boy's face. I smiled inside, accepted his boyhood, and allowed it to fill me with delight.

Who else but a four-year-old boy would have eggs behind his ears after all that care?

Mothers, we need to quit our endless spinning and focus on what's most important. Those stories you want to read will not be read unless you purposefully carve out time (and leave the mess for later).

The Bible verses will not get memorized unless you make it happen regardless of your otherwise full schedule.

One of the most important things about mothering is to carve out time. Make time. Otherwise life speeds by, and we end up tired, but not from the right things.

If you make time first for what's most important, other things will end up just fine—or not.

For me, one of the most important things is Bible time. It is incredibly important to me that the kids grow up being fed spiritually. I share with them how God's Word fills my own heart when I feel empty. I read to them and pray with them.

The rest of the day ends up just fine. Young lives are shaped best by heart things, not material things.

Show them that life is worth living, not for perfection but for blessing.

Rather than try to be everything for everyone, we need to slow down and remember we are already something to Someone.

We need to show our kids that *Someone* is much more important than *something*.

We can try our best, but little boys will still have eggs behind their ears, carry bugs into the house, and spill their milk. Just remember in all of life, *being is more important than doing.*

Father, thank You that it is not I who live, but You Who live in me. Help me to simply be with You.

DAY 67

Finally, all of you, have unity of mind, sympathy, brotherly love, a tender heart, and a humble mind. (1 Peter 3:8, ESV)

My youngest son looked at me with *that look,* and let the words out with that pouty little tone he acquires when all is not well in his little boy world.

"Mom, this is too much!"

I looked at his page and noticed he was being asked to copy eight words. He felt done at four. Often, I allow him to cut down on the amount of problems, but this morning I knew that cutting down on the amount would also cut down the amount of diligence he acquired in his growing years.

I also knew I couldn't just shut him down and make him do it, attitude and all. I'd been learning that at least giving his feelings credit goes a long way in adjusting attitude. Isn't that what I want as an adult?

I look at my son, and pause. "Tell me how you're feeling?"

He begins to whine again, "This is *toooooo much.* "

"No whining, son," I tell him. "Just talk to me about it. Quit slouching and sit up."

He sits straight and begins again, this time in a clear voice, "There are too many words to copy."

"Are you feeling overwhelmed?" I asked.

He nods his head.

"Sometimes when we feel overwhelmed, we still need to finish something. Sometimes it's really hard. But if you hurry with these words, you can finish in about five minutes," I encourage him.

He brightens up and does it at lightning speed.

Your child needs your understanding more than he needs your permissiveness. Empathizing with your child doesn't necessarily mean giving in to your child.

You can be entirely empathetic without giving up the virtues you want to teach your child. Showing empathy allows you to teach them even better because they feel heard and cared for.

A few minutes later he looks at me brightly. "I did it, Mom!"

We high-five and I drive the point home. "See? You can do hard things when you're diligent!"

He runs off to play while I sit, pondering child training and its various effects on children. I see mothers barely able to deny a child or require prompt obedience. I see these kids confident but unruly, causing unrest and disorder in atmospheres that would otherwise be peaceful. In contrast, I see kids taught to heed each word from a strict parent's lips, and I hear quick scoldings over the slightest misbehavior. I see the silent resistance on these growing kids' faces.

Rebellion occurs on both sides of the spectrum, so merely becoming tolerant isn't the solution, and neither is merely being stricter.

The solution is found in a beautiful blend of empathy and a refusal to tolerate disobedience, a combination of tough love, and love so tender it can empathize with the smallest or oldest child's emotions at any given moment.

Kids crave relationship. *Require obedience from your child, but show empathy to your child.* Give your command, then give your verbal understanding of his feelings.

If you can do both, if you can not waver in requiring obedience but can, in the process, show empathy, you have a powerful combination that most kids cannot resist.

Don't be afraid to address the feelings of a child expressing, "This is too much." Then, don't be afraid to strengthen his endurance by requiring him to finish.

And lastly, don't be afraid to high-five when it's over! Always cheer your child on to goodness!

Lord Jesus, help us treat our children with as much empathy as we treat our friends. Help us lean down to listen in. Help us lead them to the Father heart of God by showing them the heart of the Father.

Day 68

More than that, we rejoice in our sufferings, knowing that suffering produces endurance, and endurance produces character, and character produces hope. (Romans 5:3–4, ESV)

I think I've found the cure.

Running upstairs in the morning to wake four unwilling risers began to fill me with the dread people must feel when they face the beginning of their first Spartan obstacle course. It was the hardest part of the day.

I placed a lot of pressure on my own performance. Maybe if I sang a song, they would rise cheerfully; perhaps talking to them about something fun that was happening that day would work.

"Mom," they groan, "I'm too tired."

"I hate how you wake us."

"I don't want to get up."

And because I love mornings, it's all I can do not to sing loudly, pull toes, banter, and grab at covers. They groan all the more.

One morning I called the kids, but five minutes later they were still smothered in blankets. I was so weary of cajoling, baiting, and begging, that I ran downstairs and grabbed my water-filled squirt bottle. A few light mists onto their faces rewoke them immediately, and after a few mornings, my dilemma was solved. The kids responded, and my begging ended.

I can now peacefully wake each child, walk out of the room, and grab my coffee with a smile on my face. How in the world did I not see this sooner?

Sometimes we need to do the tough thing in order to spare them from tougher things later on. Response, respect, and obedience are vital elements to parenting that are fast diminishing in today's world.

A formerly opioid-addicted mother I know now helps other addicts get free like she is. "I needed someone to give me tough love," she says. "Someone who wouldn't love me to death."

Get that? Someone who wouldn't love her to death.

Parents, we can "love" our kids so much that we don't show them the right kind of love. We can be so busy protecting them that they end up unprotected from the vices of their own human hearts.

I take my kids to a homeless feeding program and let them watch. They serve napkins and mop the floor, all the while observing the destitute state of people. They see glassy eyes, wet clothing, and watch them leave in the rain with no home to go to.

When the last man comes in late, desperate for warmth and food, they watch us hand him hot soup and let him walk over the freshly mopped floor. They dump the mop water and leave with me, watching another person standing drenched in the rain.

An older gentleman says to me, "Bring your children here so they see what not to do. Let them see what happens." I nod my head, yet realize that many people suffer from homelessness due to life-altering circumstances beyond their control. Not everyone can help the fact that their finances were swept out from under their feet. But I listen, because the gentleman wants to spare my children from making bad choices.

Take your kids with you. Let them see, know, and experience while under your care the negative side of the world. Allow them to see the nasty side of things while safely under your wings.

Kids get up when they know the squirt bottle's coming. They join in the morning routine if they know there's an extra meal of dishes to wash should they choose to be lazy.

Kids need us to see what they need, and be strong enough to enforce it. Even the gentlest mother can do this. You don't need to yell, get mean or loud, or lose your cool; you simply need to exercise a little tough love with kindness and calm control.

The opioid addict knew the truth, and she wished someone else knew. As long as she was coddled, she would continue destroying herself. But when a wise, loving person no longer coddled her, she was willing to change.

Make only good things comfortable. *If a child is not in a good place, ruffle the nest.* Make obedience associated with comfort, and laziness and disobedience with discomfort. Your child will soon choose obedience if you remain consistent, calm, and loving.

Begging is for beggars—not mothers who want to wear their badge with honor. Your child will respond more to quiet, firm consequences than he will to years of cajoling and pleading. Consistent consequences can gain you years of peace, which is the first essential ingredient of a home well kept.

This type of training only works with an abundance of love and care. In fact, if you stay calm, give consequences, and hand out extravagant love, your kids will love you more, not less, than if you didn't stick with your word.

Kids subconsciously want to know there is something to respect in the person they call "Mother."

Hug a lot, laugh a lot, pray a lot, and your child will see, soon enough, a balanced blend all encompassed in one word he is able to understand: *love.*

As Os Guinness asks, "Will we have courage in a world of advanced modernity?"

Lord Jesus, help us be faithful to bring character to our children's lives by requiring them to do hard things. Help us love them in ways that are both strong and tender.

Day 69

For each will have to bear his own load. (Galatians 6:5, ESV)

What about giving our children more control?

This one grabs at our hearts. It's difficult to let go at all, let alone know when or how much to let go.

We ask ourselves what to do when a child won't comply, won't accept responsibility, refuses to do chores, and disrespects parents and siblings.

I want us to look at a new definition of control—that is, the ultimate control that also allows us to stay in control!

You cannot force a child to comply, but you can control yourself. If your child is belligerent, remind him that you have no obligation to pay for cell phones, drive to special classes, or arrange anything fun while he refuses to play his part in a well-kept home.

Give him limits, areas of life that you are unwilling to have him walk over. Respect yourself enough to refuse to tolerate his disrespect. If he persists, you also persist in your requests. If he doesn't respond, you remove your favors to him.

By placing boundaries for yourself, you are giving your older child ultimate control. Explain to him that he is now is charge of his life, though perhaps not in the way he wants or expects.

The choice is his. He can choose whether or not he will have a pleasant life or a difficult one. He is in control.

My daughter called me one day with the same complaint about her sister that she'd given two previous days. I had already given her instructions on how to handle the situation and I sucked in my breath, not wanting to go over it repeatedly. I decided to put my newly discovered method to practice.

"Hon, I don't want to spend my time hearing the same thing all over again, so I charge $50 per session," I said.

"Really, Mom?" she asked. "Can I just say one sentence? And can it be a run-on sentence?"

We burst out laughing. "Yes, child, one run-on sentence free of charge," I complied.

She got to say her piece with me being in control of what I was willing to put myself through all over again. She felt heard and I felt in control—all while giving her control of her own choices. She could either repeatedly bring up the same thing and weary her mama, or she could submit her heart to my leadership. If she did weary me, I charged $50.

Don't ever give the charge if you won't follow through. Say what you mean and do it—*every single time.* If your child refuses to pay, sell her laptop, phone, or make her buy her own things until her debt is paid.

Giving your child two options that both work for you gives your child freedom and choice while you stay in complete control. For many kids, especially growing adolescent kids, this method works much better than saying, "Quit talking *now*, or you'll get consequences!"

You will be able to breathe again when you place yourself in a breathable zone. No mother is meant to be dragged around by her own child. No mother can hold up well under the stress of nagging and cajoling a child into responsibility.

Remember the water bottle wake-up solution? My children were in charge of their mornings but not in the way they wanted. They were simply in charge of whether or not they got a spray of misty water on their faces. Obviously they wanted to be in charge in a different way by staying in bed as late as they wanted, and finishing school at 11:00 p.m. I was not about to have that.

The road to peace started with me as their mother.

Christ never admitted us into His family without the required repentance and trust in His grace. If He turned a blind eye and gave us all the benefits of His children without us coming to Him in faith, He would lose credibility as God.

In the same manner, we lose credibility as respectable parents when we tolerate and reward negative and even rebellious behavior.

The story is told of one father who couldn't wait until his child turned eighteen so he could ask him to leave. Wearied of tension, the father asked his son to leave on the morning of his eighteenth birthday.

His son was so shocked and distressed that his life turned around immediately. He became willing to honor his parents and was able to stay. As a result, there was peace and a growing relationship between father and son.

The strength and justice of God is part of what makes Him God. If He turned a blind eye to sin so that we could remain "happy" and He could be "loved," we would all know there is not as much to God as we thought there was.

So would the devil. Chaos would reign, and sin would have the final say.

But because God has standards, we get to enjoy ultimate rest in His peace, love, and righteousness. God has no space for anything else. He wins us with love, but His love is neither passive nor permissive. Because of this, His love brings freedom as we choose Him.

God is God, and He is good.

We are parents, and are asked to represent God and His attributes to our children. Yet many times we tolerate and allow an atmosphere of chaos and rebellion.

In wanting to show "mercy," we end up depriving them of true mercy and freedom.

Though we cannot force our child, we can remove privileges from his life to motivate him to choose life for himself. When he sees the consequences of his ways, he is much more willing to choose the good so he can get back to favorable living.

A choice to take his own way or get the consequences laid out for him will cause him to rethink his actions and make him want to change more than years of cajoling will.

You will be at peace, and he will be brought to peace. Even if he has seasons of rebellion, you may still walk in the peace you've created for yourself by refusing to buy into his control tactics.

It is our job as parents to raise adults who add to the world rather than take more from it.

Father, rather than try in vain to control others, help us control ourselves. Help us know that by placing our own limits, we lead our children to need to make good choices if they don't want the consequence sure to follow. Give us wisdom in our strategy.

Day 70

Give, and it shall be given to you; good measure, pressed down, shaken together, running over, will be put into your lap. (Luke 6:38, ESV)

It was Monday morning, and my little buddy woke up early as usual, soon asking the common question, "Mom, can I get on Amazon?"

"Sure, but keep the laptop on my desk," I replied sleepily from my bed.

I loved the desk view from my bed, where each day I could be reminded that I was fully equipped for all God wanted me to do. My bedroom had become a haven, one I walked into for rest and writing.

Every mom needs a haven. And apparently, every child needs a laptop to browse Amazon with. I joined him soon, squishing into the chair with him as I looked at his world of wished-for Lego sets.

Every frugal bone in my body said "no." I had bills to pay and a business to build. I didn't have to worry about finances, but I did anyway. Being on my own for the first time in my life had its mental roadblocks to overcome, even when God showed Himself faithful every single day.

I'd lay in bed thinking about those bills. But more importantly, I'd lay there thinking about my children. How could I give the four of them the best life possible, not just in providing for them, but in studying them, what they were good at, and what they needed in order to grow into their own talents and strengths?

How could I occupy them with goodness?

There were 951 teeny pieces in this Lego set. I knew it would give my son many, many hours of productive, brain-expanding play. He was a nerdy little fellow who could fix all kinds of things by the age of nine. He loved technology and a hundred times a day I said no to more screen time while I guided him to other things.

But I couldn't say no to the things he loved unless I filled it with other things he also loved. So, I drew a deep breath and hit that infamous "place in cart" icon.

I spent the next hour worrying that I'd done the wrong thing. But mothers, we can't put our growing sons in stagnant places. Children are wired to expand their horizons, experience the world, and go places. As early as nine years old, my son needed to be well-occupied or he'd get bored. And boredom is one of the greatest causes of trouble.

The pool in the backyard offered him water and exercise on hot days when the chores were done and he didn't know what to do with himself. The trampoline offered exercise and soon became part of his chore list where I'd write, "Put clean dishes away" right along with, "Jump on trampoline one hundred times."

Mothers, we need to study our children. When you see a child with the capability of becoming a video game couch potato, you work against that from a young age by purposefully placing better things right before them.

Allow your children to see goodness. Many moms say no without saying yes, and many adults spend each breath talking down on the evil in this world but are too lazy to engage in the goodness all around them.

Bringing goodness to our children takes time, effort, energy, and yes, *money*.

Frugality is a virtue; deprivation is not.

It's easy to drag through each day without doing what it takes to pull the goodness right into our child's ordinary day.

I want to remind us that even we, as mothers, need to see the goodness of God in order to stay away from the evil of this world. I can only say no to lesser things when I realize I'm saying yes to better things.

Jesus said, "My food is to do the will of Him who sent me, and to finish His work" (John 4:34, ESV). Jesus's task on Earth was a difficult one, but He was able to finish it faithfully because He had utter trust in the goodness of God.

Our children live in a difficult world. They can only believe in the goodness of God when they begin to taste it for themselves. We bring this to them in a multitude of ways, starting very young.

Yesterday, I wrapped my arms around my children during church services. Then, we went out to eat with some friends. I purposefully shared with them what the sermon meant to me as we drove. That night I gave my son a massage on the table when he had a headache, and took a walk with my daughter in the cool evening air. All of this gave opportunities to talk about things on their hearts.

It really doesn't matter if some of them don't want to do what we're doing. Our job as parents is to lead them there, *anyway.* Most children won't choose to end the day with Bible time—but it's up to us to nourish their souls just as we nourish their bodies.

From Legos to beaches to Bible time to church services, all of it plays a part. So does your pocketbook.

Every once in a while, when you can, say yes to something your child wants that will be good for him. Engage in your child's world so he will engage his ear to your voice.

Father, thank You for your goodness. Thank You for leading us to Yourself by showing us that all Your ways are absolutely perfect. In a broken world, help us put forth the energy and time to bring as much of Your good to our children as possible.

DAY 71

Delight yourself in the Lord and He will give you the desires of your heart.
(Psalm 37:4, ESV)

Though slightly embarrassed to do so at my age, I bent low over my birthday cake and made a silent wish.

My son pulled at my shirt. "Mom, tell me what your wish is!"

"Birthday wishes are private," I told him.

He kept asking to speak with me so I followed him into another room and bent my ear to his lips. "I know what your wish is. You wish we children would stay little forever and live at home for the rest of our lives."

I smiled. That hadn't been my wish, but I was grateful my little boy felt loved and he saw what my true values were. He and his siblings were my greatest priority as a single mother, and he knew it.

My child studied his mother unawares. And now, we need to study our children on purpose and ask ourselves what they see in us.

Find in them your own reflection. Then study the Father's heart for yourself and make sincere changes based on everything He shows you.

Our kids are not our own possession; they are God's. They deserve our respect and the greatest effort we can give because they are worth just as much as we are.

We were once children. *Let's see them as human beings placed here with us for a reason greater than ourselves.* Let's help them see their value to the Lord by placing high value on them.

Let's listen to their feelings even when it seems annoying.

Let's consider their changing needs and make adjustments accordingly.

Let's give up and give in when love calls us to do so.

When it doesn't matter, let's change our rules for their sake.

Show them love and life, and they will be more likely to follow your rules and guidelines.

God always parents us with both. We trust Him because He is just. We worship Him because He is full of goodness. We love Him because He loved us first. He is our greatest comfort and our highest Lord at the same time.

This is why parenting without really knowing Him can end in so much disaster. God created our kids to need every aspect of Himself.

They see Him first and foremost in Mama.

Study your children, but most of all, study who God is and what He is to you. Make a wish on your birthday or every day, and know that God means to fill your soul as you align yourself to His heart.

Lord Jesus, help us contemplate each day what our children see in us, what they would most associate us with. Help us be the person we want them to see when they think of us. And help us to delight ourselves in You, trusting that You know the desires of our hearts.

DAY 72

Whatever you do, work heartily, as for the Lord and not for men.
(Colossians 3:23, ESV)

The kids swung their rags through the air just as I did many years ago when my mother placed a cleaning rag in my hand. We turned on the music and for a few hours we polished, scrubbed, swept, and mopped this house that's seen a merry, messy week.

I remember the days when they were all little and I took to cleaning myself. Bathroom, kitchen, and bedrooms faced my determined rag—because once a week, I thoroughly conquered the awful mess my little angels created.

My mother was one of those immaculate people who swept the kitchen floor three times a day and cleaned under beds once a week. Dust wads must have panicked in her house. Bi-yearly we'd move furniture and take beds apart to wash every part of the frame.

I learned to love clean. Really clean.

Then I had four children who taught me to relax at night and leave dishes on the counter. For a while, my stomach refused to digest its dinner at the thought of the mess waiting for me the next morning. But I learned that happy children are worth more than a pristine kitchen—and sometimes, both won't happen.

Mothers can't always give time to people and immaculate living at the same time. Dishes wait, but people learn quickly what's most important to Mama.

But then, the kids grew a little. And a little more. Soon they were old enough to push a mop and swing a rag, but they hated it just as I did when my own mother taught me. I persisted. Then, I insisted. "Everyone eats, sleeps, and uses the toilet around here," I declared. "And each of you will pitch in as long as you live here."

Friday became the day. With one child scrubbing the bathroom, another sweeping out bedrooms, and Mama scouring the kitchen, it was done in a few hours. I chose to ignore complaints and require diligence. I chose to hush nagging, including my own.

Week after week, we stuck to it—and then, one day it struck me. I had an eleven-year-old son begging me to allow him to get his cleaning done. "Mama, may I clean tonight so I don't have to tomorrow?"

What boy asks to get it done? The next week he formulated a list, mapping out each chore needing to be accomplished and naming who would do it. I was fascinated. Here I had an eleven-year-old who hated work planning the most efficient way to get it done *because he knew he had to.*

If I hadn't stuck to it, he'd be on the couch wiling the day away. He's naturally a lazy child, but he's fast becoming a hardworking young man. And it didn't just happen by chance.

Mark your kids' days with routine. Work chores into their schedule in the same way you work mealtime, bedtime, playdates, and other things. Allow them to have fun *after chores are through*, rather than filling their days with fun because you are loathe to require anything else.

If you stick to it, they will learn that fun happens if and when those chores are accomplished. They will start making it happen on their own because Mama won't rescue them from unfulfilled duty, neither will she plan a playdate for the weekend until they're through.

Let's create willing workers who will bless society long after we are done training them!

Father, give us wisdom on how to bring our children into our work at a young age, and teach them that work is part of life even as play is. Help us bring laughter into chores. Help us bring them through chores even when laughter is the last thing on their minds, teaching them that not all of life can be fun.

DAY 73

Love is patient and kind; love does not envy or boast; it is not arrogant or rude. It does not insist on its own way; it is not irritable or resentful; it does not rejoice at wrongdoing, but rejoices with the truth.

Love bears all things, believes all things, hopes all things, endures all things. (1 Corinthians 13:4–7, ESV)

"She hurt my feelings."

"I feel left out."

"She goes to her house more than she comes to mine."

Navigating girl friendships with my two daughters brought me more stress than many things in life. I found myself paddling to stay above the mucky waters of keeping everyone happy. Who wants to hurt someone's feelings?

I'd make my daughters do things that stressed them out just so another mother wouldn't get upset. I'd book our schedule too full just to include everyone in our week. Life was one flurry of running here and there, of having other kids in our home, of wanting everyone to feel loved.

I love letting others know I love them. And when you love on a mother's child, you love on her. I wanted my friends to know that I cared about them. But I also wanted everyone's approval and I was working hard to keep it.

The pressure I felt wore on me, and I soon learned that I needed to slow down. I learned to decline invitations and not bring guests home at certain times.

And then, one of my friends showed one of the greatest displays of wisdom I'd ever seen in a mother. Her daughter was quiet, unassuming, and gracious to all. I soon learned why her daughter displayed character as she did.

This girl's brother was best friends with my son and they hung out a lot. My daughter's schedule was more full than my son's, so the girls didn't hang out as often as the boys did.

Rather than be hurt, this girl's mother taught her not to expect love in the way she wants it, but to receive it in the way it's given. In her own words, "My mother and grandmother taught me that you cannot love someone on your terms. If you want a relationship, you have to love them on theirs. So, if you only receive love one way and expect everyone to bend to that, you're not really loving them.

"However, my mother also taught me that you have boundaries. If the other person is manipulating you to 'love them in their way or you are wrong,' boundaries are good and needed. It's a mix of love, understanding, respect, and communicating.

"Do we always get it right?" she continued. "No way, but relationships are work. The best relationships sometimes go through very hard times and come out better in the end. It's work, and very worth it."

Her daughter is fortunate to have a mother who teaches her hands-on love. Her daughter won't be using people to fill her own agenda, but will understand that there's a place to fit in the lives of others—and it doesn't always look like our version of love.

In the long run, fitting into others' lives like her daughter did into ours is love in the deepest sense. She was willing to have less than she wanted because she learned to care about another's life as well. She learned to receive the time given rather than feel hurt that not more time was available.

As a grown woman, I'm still learning about receiving love in the way it's given.

When this girl is grown and married, she will already have learned to receive graciously what is offered her. She will have more realistic expectations than most and will be content whether she's in the limelight or not. She will love genuinely, and receive genuine love.

She is, after all, the rare fourth generation of wise women who believe that you cannot force others to love you on your terms, but must learn to receive love as it's given. For four generations, these ladies have been taught to believe that when you pressure others to love you in your own way, it's not really love at all.

When my daughter has less time to hang out than this friend would like, she is able to respect that rather than compare, complain, and manipulate someone into having her over as often as she would like.

Perhaps if all of us taught ourselves and our daughters this kind of love, we'd hear less of, "I feel left out," and "She hurt my feelings."

Perhaps mothers would feel free to plan small birthday parties rather than large ones "so everyone could be included."

Love gives more than it gets.

Love thinks about another.

Love doesn't envy.

And love is always, always happy for someone who is rejoicing.

Love is all about caring for another's need more than your own desires. Love can ask for something it desires, but graciously yield to another when it's not possible for someone to give it.

Love gives to another more than it uses another.

When love is fully known in the heart, it extends itself more than it grasps for itself.

Let's teach our daughters what my wise mama friend did. I'm honored to know her and glean wisdom by her hearth, from her heart, in her home.

Lord, help us teach our children not to victimize themselves over unmet expectations, but to have a deep sense of self-worth that can't be thrown off by another person's life. Help us give them security so they are not constantly looking for it in a crowd or person. Help us teach them how to love others well more than seek to be loved a certain way.

DAY 74

You make known to me the path of life; in your presence there is fullness of joy; at your right hand are pleasures forevermore. (Psalm 16:11, ESV)

I woke to the sound of pouring rain, and my heart sank. The fundraiser bake sale! It couldn't be done in rain, and there were piles of goodies on the counter waiting to be sold at the neighbor's yard sale that day.

The kids had worked for hours, and I knew that God knew. He saw them bake so they could give to refugees their auntie was working with.

The rain subsided just in time to set up, and they all displayed the treats on the table, sat down for the morning, and waited. As I checked in, the oldest daughter said, "Mama, when we don't have customers, I pray, and they come."

The kids waited on customers for hours that day, and in the end were thrilled with their earnings for the displaced people of Syria. But here is the best part of this little story: as soon as the last load of baked goods were carried back inside, rain started pouring again.

We were awed. The kids saw God that day in all the beauty of relationship.

Teach your kids about relationship by bringing God into every aspect of their lives. We are born to be inhabited and be fully known.

When we are inhabited, we are hosting His presence. Hosting His presence in our hearts is entirely different than thinking religious thoughts in our head.

The devil believes, and trembles. He knows that Jesus exists and came to save mankind. But he has no presence dwelling in him.

We first know God through repentance and faith. Repentance is a gift, not a curse. Humbling oneself is a blessing. Both are to pull us into relationship. Both heart postures affect and change our outward behavior.

God gives us freedom, then draws us back to Himself by showing us what a mess we are without His presence. As Danny Silk says in *Loving Our Kids on Purpose*, "Without the freedom to reject Him, we are powerless to choose Him."

Choosing to say, "I can't live a righteous life" brings you to the greatest strength you could ever know. Turning away from all you are to all Christ is allows you to experience the indwelling Christ. He abides with those who surrender and trust each and every day.

When He abides, He does His work. This is why true saving faith actually changes you, truly saves you from yourself.

It all begins on the inside, by faith. It happens in relationship and nowhere else.

Are we merely thinking religious thoughts, or are we hosting His presence? In the same way, do we merely teach our kids to obey, or do we get into their hearts so they choose and want to obey?

When you punish behavior but fail to address the root that caused the behavior, you miss out on the heart and spend a lot of time trying to do away with symptoms.

As Danny Silk says, "If I can deal with my child's attitude, I will have far less behavior to deal with."

Of course there are many times when we need to require obedience regardless of where the heart is. But our main job as a parent is to establish a relationship with our kids and hold their hearts with our own. From that premise, prompt obedience will happen much sooner.

Show your children that in God's presence is joy!

As God showed Himself to my children the day of their bake sale, so we mothers can show ourselves to our children just by showing up every day and leading them to see God in all things.

Use rain on the day of a bake sale to bring them to prayer and dependence. Watch God move each day and speak of it often. If you do, you will most likely start to hear it from their lips as well!

Father, show me how to lead my children right into Your presence long before eternity.

DAY 75

The LORD is my shepherd; I shall not want. He makes me lie down in green pastures. He leads me beside still waters. He restores my soul. He leads me in paths of righteousness for his name's sake.

Even though I walk through the valley of the shadow of death, I will fear no evil, for you are with me; your rod and your staff, they comfort me. (Psalm 23:1–4, ESV)

What about that child who *simply refuses* to obey no matter how much you love on him?

Like, when you ask a child to keep his room cleaned up, and he just won't. Or, you ask a child not to be on her phone for only a short time, *but she's always on it?*

I can run myself ragged with reminders, or I can quietly give a consequence. This week, it looked like this:

"Kids, I've asked you to keep your clothes picked up. I've been saying the same thing over and over, yet there are constant piles left on your floor. From now on, if you leave clothes on the floor in the morning, I will bag them up and put them in the storage shed outside where you'll have to haul them back inside when you want to wear them."

Of course I had to follow through and listen to some excuses. I had to listen, then quietly let her be angry. I also had to do a repeat the next day.

Hauling heavy bags of clothes wasn't fun. The second and third day I was still hauling three garbage bags of clothes to the shed. But on the fourth day she had no clothes on the floor.

I'm asking myself, "What am I afraid of?"

My own kids' disapproval, or what? Because living like this means I'm out of control, not in control, and kids can sense fear and timidity like a dog senses bloody meat.

My journey into strength didn't lead me out of all fear. I'm the mother who loves her children to death but wants to die when conflict happens. I'm also the mother who now realizes that it's OK for my child to be unhappy with me. I'm the one who knows beyond doubt that God loves me and has my back. That it's unrealistic to expect all children to love my decision-making at all times.

But hey, we feel like that should be reality.

Brace up, Mama—it's just not. And that's OK, believe it or not.

It's OK for your children to struggle. Most of them do, and some of them go through very difficult times. Many children who don't struggle with outwardly rebellious behavior struggle with inner vices.

I know I did. I was the good child. But, I struggled with condemnation and fear as much or more than children who struggle with anger or other more apparent things. Both are vices from the enemy meant to drive us away from the Father's love.

We are so insanely *human*. Can you walk with your child without needing to perfect your child? Can you give him space to sort life out, to learn, to be human on this earth where heaven has not yet taken over?

Your children are not your identity; God is. When a good mother has a struggling child (and I've seen many of them), she is not to blame. The same mother can have a near-perfect child, having used the same parenting techniques with both.

Of course we always search our hearts and repent of mistakes when we notice a struggling child. This alone is a gift because only love leads us to repentance and change. There is nothing as motivating for changing our own needs and faults as a struggling child.

In the end, we give our hearts and love as best we know how. We choose to grow, we ask counsel, we pray. But God wants us free from fear and condemnation, able to walk with Him hand in hand knowing how much we are loved.

Mothers, one of the best things we can give our children is peace. Walk with your child down valleys or up mountains—just walk with him and with God, and be at peace, knowing God loves your child more than you do and is able to work miracles that even our best efforts can't attain.

I never felt the love of Jesus more than when I needed to walk with my children through their own valleys. Mothering is all about knowing each dynamic of love—both receiving and giving it.

Whether it's a picking-up-the-clothes issue or something much, much bigger, give yourself grace as you face more difficulties than expected and don't know what to do. Breathe, pray, be at peace, and extend that same peace to your children as you seek God for kingdom solutions.

Father, thank You for walking with us so very closely during hard times. For showing us that parenting isn't about perfection but about being swallowed up in Your perfect love. Thank You that our identity is in You.

Day 76

Let all that you do be done in love. (1 Corinthians 16:14, ESV)

"This is Satan!" my little boy's eyes twinkled merrily.

He held a spoon into a mixer on high speed and watched it hit, clatter, and bang. I laughed and just let him do it.

It wasn't long ago that he smashed twenty-seven anthills on one walk with his mama and pretended that Satan had to be in the swarm of biting ants. Somewhere along the way he'd picked up that Satan is a very evil spirit and he was in an all-out war against him.

He reminded me of how I felt when I walked with my children through things I never thought I'd face as a parent. Something rises inside a mother's heart when a child faces trials of such magnitude that they push him into a dark place.

I'll never forget how Jesus met me there, walking alongside my child and assuring me of His love.

How He taught me that purpose, not perfection, was the goal in mothering.

How he assured me it was OK to have struggling children and it is a very real part of parenting.

How He reminded me of his great love for less-than-perfect women when he chose Mary Magdalene to run to the city with news of his resurrection.

In times of great struggle with my child, I found great love from my God.

Back to my little boy. A few days later he wants to know how we can best trick Satan.

"By listening to God when Satan's trying to trick you," I told him.

We talked almost the entire hour-and-a-half drive as his little mind tried to grasp the deeper things of life and God. My heart soared, and it was one of those rewarding, "I'm being a really good mom" moments. The drive went by quickly as I engaged his tender, curious mind.

Enter about eight hours later on the way home, when it was dark and we were both exhausted. Grumpy and tired, he complained until he fell asleep in the back seat of the car.

I felt like a terrible mother. My poor child was tired and unhappy and I couldn't fix it.

I'm always trying to "fix it" for my children. The little tyke loses two quarters to an unwilling toy machine and I'm making up for it by taking him to Dunkin' and letting him inhale a cream-filled, chocolate-frosted pastry almost as large as his face.

Nothing thrills me as much as a happy child. But alone in the car as I wove through traffic and tried to get him home to bed as soon as possible, I realized it all over again.

The purpose of parenting was never perfection. I wasn't a better mother when all was well on the drive up and I wasn't a terrible mother when he was tired and grumpy on the way home before he fell asleep. I was simply a mother loving my child with all my heart and doing my best with him that day.

It's easier to say with a little tyke, but it's true of our teens, too. Mothers, that ache in your soul when you watch your teen struggle and can't do anything about it—give it to God and allow Him to love you. Then, extend the same toward your child.

God never wanted your perfect life as much as He wanted you to see the purpose for your life.

This earth is made of spiritual war and bloodshed, which means there are long and sometimes ugly battles to fight. Don't expect anything less for something as precious as the soul of your child.

Expect an easy route and you'll be thrown off guard.

Expect a battle and you'll find grace through the struggle.

Make sure you love your child *unconditionally, where no sacrifice it too great and no amount of struggle dissolves your love.* Find ways to show your child that your love remains the same because your purpose in parenting is not his perfection for the sake of your own image.

Mothers, we must let go of this perfection thing. Life is real and struggles will come, sometimes very long, great ones. **Embrace the struggle and embrace your child.**

Smile when your little boy wants to beat the devil up like a spoon in a mixer. Then, do that very thing by taking Jesus with you into every place of struggle or success where you find His love as your identity. The presence of Jesus is your most powerful weapon, and He wins you with His love. Lean into His love so you won't crash from your trials.

Lord Jesus, thank You that You never asked or expected me to bring perfection into each moment. Life is full of both ease and difficulty, and my job as a mother isn't to keep all difficulty out of my child's life. Help me to give him all my love through each moment, whether easy or difficult.

DAY 77

Rejoice always, pray without ceasing, give thanks in all circumstances; for this is the will of God in Christ Jesus for you. (1 Thessalonians 5:16–18, ESV)

I crawled onto my little boy's floor bed and asked him for the hundredth time, "Why are you sleeping on the hard floor in Mama's room when you have a nice bed in a boy's room?"

He'd grin sheepishly and we both knew the answer. He loved Mama's bed, but his recent birthday graduated him from the privilege of sleeping in it. So, he opted for the floor beside Mama's bed.

"What was the best part of your day?" I asked him.

"Nothing," he said.

I smiled in the dark and knew there had been a hundred good things in his day, but his natural tendency toward pessimism and perfection overrode any positive vibe when he was asked to remember something good.

I walked him through his day. "You had friends to play with, you had good school to do, you had ice cream . . . and you get to fall asleep feeling thankful for all the good things in your life."

My little boy can have an entire day full of parties and gifts, yet focus on the one thing that annoyed him. He's a loner and perfectionist—and go figure, crowds are loud and imperfect. Some of us just happen to love that while others don't.

I'm walking him through complaints to gratitude. "It's OK not to like something," I tell him. "But we can always choose things to be thankful for even if there are some things we don't like."

This attitude starts with us, mothers. But it doesn't mean we deny our trials; it means we're grateful in spite of our trials. *Life will never be perfect but it can always be full of wonder.*

I say this to my little boy, too. I want him to know he can talk about things he doesn't like, but our main focus will be gratitude. I want to reprogram his negativism to the positive because I believe it will impact him for the rest of his life.

It's amazing how much joy can be picked up when you focus on the good. Remember, eternity will be spent celebrating all things good and the only One truly good. This good God is already with us!

Lead your child to a good God who showers him daily with good things. Use every opportunity to show him goodness! Guide him toward gratitude while embracing the hard things, too.

Always hear him, then lead him.

I cherish these moments when he asks to snuggle up. And I don't just cherish them—I use them. We are in an all-time battle for the souls of our children and the war is fought best with strategies of *goodness* pulling the souls of our children toward God.

Lord Jesus, thank You that I get to fill my child's day with goodness, then pull him toward Your goodness by being thankful for each gift You gave him through the day. Help us know that gratitude doesn't mean denial of the hard; it just means being thankful for the good even when there are hard things.

Day 78

I will open my mouth in a parable . . . things that we have heard and known, that our fathers have told us.

We will not hide them from our children, but tell to the coming generation the glorious deeds of the Lord, and his might, and the wonders that he has done. (Psalm 78:2–4, ESV)

"Do you hear that weird noise coming from the car?" I asked my daughter. "Hear that?"

We drove a few miles farther, turned around due to a venue change, and decided to pull over as the noise intensified. A busy exit had me hopping out warily to discover a popped front tire.

Simultaneous relief that it was only a popped tire and dread flooded my mind as I stood there, trucks whizzing past on the busy exit leading to the freeway. It was hot, very hot—and I didn't know how to change a tire.

What's more, I was new in town and didn't know very many people. I made a few calls when I noticed a white car pull over ahead of us and ease down closer to us.

It was my daughter's friend whom I had just tried to call. He had no idea we were stranded on the side of the road and just "happened" to pass by.

Southern sun can be so hot it sends shivers right up your spine. But the young man knelt into the gravel with bare knees and sweated away for an hour, all the while teaching my daughter and I how to do exactly what he was doing for us.

I looked at my daughter. "There really is a God, Sweetie. He cares for us, always."

It had been anything but easy for both of us when her father left and gave his attention and life to another girl. Daily, I asked God for strength as I watched my children struggle to work through abandonment and betrayal.

Every day, eight large eyes filled with sadness that only people who've been through the same thing can know. Every day, I tried to lead them on to goodness, hope, and trust that God would never fail us even if people did. And often I asked God to bring his people into my children's lives in a deeply personal way.

This young man had been reaching out to my children and it was no coincidence that he was the one God sent to help us. His mother had passed away a few years before, and I knew she'd be proud of her son as he sacrificed his volleyball game for a stranded mom and her daughter.

Some mother left a legacy when she was long gone.

I stared at the trees as more cars went whizzing by. The sun blazed down with intensity but all was OK. God had shown up once again, just as He had a million times over in the last two years.

I always told my children when God's care showed itself, and it happened very, very often. Unexpected gifts straight from heaven when they were needed most. Sometimes gifts of money, other times needed words of encouragement, other times small things like a box of skincare products, or even an older widow asking if I could help her eat an abundance of chicken she had cooked too much of.

The chicken wasn't a huge deal, but the fact that it happened right as I was craving chicken was the big deal—and another love sign from heaven.

My daughter was watching me that day when the tire went flat. She could tell whether or not I would give God credit or simply count it as luck.

"This was God," I told her again. "God cares for us."

Rather than push God onto our children, it is up to us to bring God to our children.

Invite Him into every aspect of life, and all of life will be worship. Serenade your children's atmosphere with Jesus Christ when they are struggling most, but do so in many practical ways more than many preachy ways.

I thanked the young man as I drove away with a spare tire gracing the side of my usually nice-looking car, picked up the youngest children, and headed to a party more than an hour late.

But everything was OK. My children saw God move that day, and I was able to invite them to gratitude to a relational, personal God Who was always with us.

Lord Jesus, thank You for being so deeply personal. Thank You for showing up over and over and over again. Thank You for being in our lives and showing Yourself to our children.

DAY 79

For thus says the Lord God, the Holy One of Israel, "In returning and rest shall you be saved; in quietness and confidence shall be your strength." (Isaiah 30:15, ESV)

"I have to fix it for them."

My emotions begged me while my rational mind blankly told me I couldn't fix it. And as is so often true, my rational mind won the race while emotions were forced to take the back seat.

COVID-19 had us all on lockdown right after we moved from the West Coast to the East. My four dear children were undergoing massive change and not a day passed by that I didn't wonder what on Earth God was up to.

You'd think the array of "stuff" would just stop, that not one more thing would hit—but then it does, anyway.

Life circumstances don't care if even law enforcement is scratching its head and calling our situation the type of story TV shows are made of. Such was our life for a few long years, and then COVID-19 was added to the mix.

I remember feeling almost desperate to change the story for my children.

I also remember knowing I could not, that all I could do was pick them up and be there for them 24/7 as we all tried to make our way through, together.

The hardest times of letting go can be when the realization hits that we are no longer in absolute control of our children's comfort.

When the children were born, I'd leap out of bed in the middle of the night five times if I had to, just to comfort that baby and let it snuggle one more time. And, I'm still holding my teens.

This idea that "training" a newly born baby to sleep all night by letting it cry wasn't even something I wanted to consider. The idea seemed abusive to me. "I'd rather be tired from getting up at night," I'd say—*and I meant every word.*

But I can't hold their life as they grow older. Sometimes it just is what it is, and these are the times to teach our children by example what it means to trust God and hang onto Him for dear life.

The Healer is always greater than the hurt.

Purpose always triumphs over pain.

Grace always wins over grief.

I'd lead them to my room at night where we'd all crowd around and read Scripture together. Some of them would undoubtedly be grouchy or tired—but this nightly routine settled their souls more than they realized.

I'd tell them of the Healer, and how God is absolutely more powerful than human mistakes.

I'd tell them of endurance and what it means to never give up.

I'd tell them of faithfulness, of how to get through one more day even when we all wanted to stay in bed and forget life for a while.

When we can't fix our children's lives, we lead them to the One who can heal their hearts.

Over and over again during those days I told my children that God never promised us perfect lives, but He did promise His perfect love throughout our lives.

When we can't remove our children's trial, let's lead them to see God through the trial.

The greatest gift we can give them is not a perfect life, but a realization of how to lean into God in every circumstance.

We live in an imperfect world while we so desperately want to give them everything perfectly. But endurance is of utmost importance if we want them to grow into adults who can show up during difficult times and make the most of life as it sometimes is.

Help your children to lean into the trial by accepting it, then lead them to lean into *grace*.

Mother, you can't fix everything. Accepting this means you open the door for the Healer to lead you to the other side. It means you get to rest when the waves still tumble and roar because you're not trying to better things outside of your control.

It means your children will have a prime example of what it looks like to love and trust Jesus when things get difficult. In this way, Mother, that massive trial you can't fix becomes a gift, a doorway, an opportunity to lead your children to see Jesus Christ.

Let your emotions be still. God is in control of the waves.

Father, You are good, and You are our Father. Thank You that when our burdens become too much for us, You bear them for us. Thank You that we don't have to fix things outside of our control but can leave them to You. Help us look for Your perfect love in the trial more than we look for a perfect life without trial.

Day 80

In peace I will both lie down and sleep, for you alone, O Lord, make me dwell in safety. (Psalm 4:8, ESV)

My child was struggling, and I was worried to a panic. What's more, I had no vision of what to do.

Every mother who's been in that place knows what I'm talking about. Those nights where you don't sleep until 3:00 a.m., that day where you can't enjoy anything because your child isn't OK, that week where everything feels twice as hard because you're worried sick.

That humbling experience of reaching out with honest tears asking for honest answers because you don't have it all together and life is very real. The days of watching the struggle prolong before the victory unfolds.

How do we carry ourselves in those days, mothers?

We may love in life, but it's for our children that we get this overwhelming mama-bear urge to make everything bad and yucky go away *at once.* Then, our children grow older and take life by the hand.

Will we go under on the bad days and up on the good ones?

Something whispered to my heart that I couldn't keep doing what I was doing, that I would lose my health, peace, and joy if I didn't let go just a little.

I prayed, and God spoke. "Sara, let your child go through this process. Allow your child to battle his way forward. Rest before you see victory."

My friend agreed. We took another one of the children to the White Water Center on a day when I could have spent hours in useless worry. I faced my water paranoia with rafting, gripped to the side of the raft, and let the boat twist backward through rapids as we all hung on for dear life. We jumped from hundred-foot towers into thin air as gravity hurled us downward. For some reason I wanted to do it twice, lean into my fear, and let go. Stepping into thin air and feeling your body drop a hundred feet takes courage, in some ways more than sky-diving had.

We played until we couldn't walk anymore, and something shifted in my soul.

Yes, my child was struggling. But there was a good God on the lookout, offering me help in time of need. There was a big, beautiful world out there to enjoy and all kinds of lovely things to focus on as I prayed and waited for breakthrough.

I pulled my tired legs into the car at the end of the day and realized the small, ugly world of struggle I had been living in. Yes, I was to bear my child's burden as I prayed and loved and stood on the side waiting to help in every way I could. *But grace was meant to overtake my soul.*

Hear this, mothers—we need to be overtaken by grace when we'd rather use worry as an underhanded weapon for our cause. *Worry never works; grace wins every time.*

Your child's lack of peace does not need to determine yours. Now more than ever, he needs to see you with the very thing his soul craves.

Every human being craves peace. Not every child is ready to do what it takes to have it. Or, in my case as a younger person, I didn't know how to have it, didn't know how loving and kind Jesus Christ was, nor how much I could trust Him. Teen years are hard, and when the struggle isn't outwardly difficult there are often internal problems. Every mother needs bravery during these times.

God wants us to utilize peace in the process of our children's purification. Our weapons are prayer, love, peace, and worship rather than fear, sleepless nights, and anxious worry.

Choose to be overtaken by God's everlasting grace as your child goes through a temporary struggle. Always allow grace to have the final say over your life whether or not your child does.

One mother who was sick with worry for her teens told me she literally had to leave her children with her husband and go take a break, learn to let go, and really live without trying to control each person around her. I love seeing her smile today as she sits beside her husband and they walk other parents through the same things. Finding her own peace before her children found theirs only enhanced the very thing she wanted. She had to let go and let God.

I gripped the raft tightly and screamed a bit (actually a lot) as rapids very nearly turned us over and my darling babe sat in the front facing waves I was too afraid to navigate. She was brave.

I could be brave, too. I needed to be brave. Long before everything ironed out, this mama needed to live in grace, because only that would help anything at all.

I slept well that night and enjoyed the following week as I watched my struggling child navigate his world. I handed out love and advice more than fear and control. When a friend asked what color my heart felt that week, I said "Yellow, because I feel the hope of sunshine."

Because of Jesus Christ, we can live in sunshine even when under cloudy skies.

All, all, all is *grace*.

Lord Jesus, thank You for loving us so much that You hand out Your gifts no matter what we're facing. Thank You for not leaving us in a place of panic, but gently leading us to peace.

Day 81

My flesh and my heart may fail, but God is the strength of my heart and my portion forever. (Psalm 73:26, ESV)

The cover fell off the book, but it only added to its character and the fact that even the title seemed a bit over-used.

Codependent No More struck me as a little stale because I'd spent the last few years realizing how absolutely codependent I had been. My mom and I discussed the subject at length and then, I mailed the book her way.

"As with everything," my note to her said, "there is meat to chew and bones to spit out. But the truth in this book is worth grabbing hold of."

Sometimes finding bones to spit out gets wearying. But I'm teaching my children that everyone and everything except Jesus Christ has issues, lacks, blind spots, and faulty areas in their lives.

I want my children to know that it's OK to be less than perfect, it's OK to be on a journey, and it's OK to embrace others who are less than perfect, too.

I grew up in a cloistered world where only those who lived and dressed and spoke and thought like we did were welcome. I wonder how many of us looked at ourselves and wondered if there were blind spots in our own lives as well? I idolized people and almost worshipped their holiness rather than being in touch with a truly holy God. And the holiness I wanted to live was a deep quest for approval from God and those around me rather than a rested heart that cannot help but live peace.

The people I idolized all showed me how human they were, and bit by bit my gaze went upward rather than outward. I soon realized that no human deserves the near-worship I wanted to give them, and that if I gave them the worship only God deserved, I would most likely be severely disappointed.

The lesson I learned about others applied to myself as well. I wasn't perfect and never would be. Others weren't perfect and they also never would be.

What a liberating fact to embrace and lead our children toward! Receive all good, reject all bad, anywhere and everywhere, from anyone and everyone. The rest is simple—*Jesus Christ gets all adoration and implicit trust.*

Raise your children with a deep awareness of the perfections of Jesus Christ, of His glorious beauty, of His majesty and worthiness. Simultaneously, speak to them about human failure and how it is never to be compared with God's goodness. This will equip them to continue trusting Jesus when those around them fail to represent Him as they should.

All humans fail.

God does not.

Seeing the perfection of Christ leads us to better process the imperfections of this world.

Rather than be blindsided and turned away from the faith when people fail us greatly, we can be tuned into the goodness of God because we've conditioned our minds to **expect failure in a fallen world while we expect goodness from a risen Christ.**

The purpose of Christ always overrides the pain of this world. Teach your children to separate the two so they can better process the failure from another human being that is sure to come at some point in their lives.

My child couldn't understand how God could let tragedy happen in my life when I loved and served Him. She watched me cry, pick myself back up, and worship Jesus. Then, she watched me do that a hundred times over.

I was so glad to tell her that I don't measure the goodness of an immortal God with the failure of mortal humans. The two are so vastly opposite they don't even compare.

A human's sin should cause us to run to God rather than run from God.

Our hurts should lead us to the Healer rather than lead us to hurt ourselves more by removing ourselves from the presence of the God of all Comfort.

Lead your children to expect faulty humans while they lean hard on a faultless savior. Teach them not to compare the two, but to worship the only Good One.

Live free!

Father, thank You that You've removed the lie from our hearts that says You must not be good if people hurt us. Thank You for setting us free to see Your goodness with the eyes of our hearts, and to allow nothing and no one to take that from us. Help us be faithful to teach our children the same so they can be strong in faith when hurts come.

DAY 82

There is therefore now no condemnation to those who are in Christ Jesus, who walk not after the flesh, but after the spirit. (Romans 8:1, ESV)

"I'm so tired, I think I just need to rest right now," I told my daughters. They nodded and agreed to do dishes and clean the kitchen. My oldest had already cooked dinner, knowing she was going to help clean afterward.

Every mother knows what it's like to be so tired you just can't move anymore. That was my state Friday night as I showered and collapsed onto my bed with a book and laptop.

Little Buddy helped with dishes, too, then joined me upstairs and crawled into bed with me where we finished off a cowboy movie. He loves to snuggle and was intrigued by the cowboys.

I'd been laying there wishing I could be more for my children. That old onslaught of "You should, you should, you should," was ringing in my head as I wished I could be laughing and talking and mingling downstairs.

Instead, I was crashed on a bed so tired I could barely even read, so I turned on the screen.

When my husband left and I started working as well as being mother to four children, tired took on a whole new meaning. I learned a lot in this season of never feeling like I could be enough for my children.

I'd walk out the door in the morning with Little Buddy being watched by his sisters. For a mom who homeschooled for many years, that's a difficult step. When school was in season, I'd walk him out to the bus at 6:35 a.m. More than one morning I choked back the tears as lights blinked away on a long yellow bus so early in the morning that it was still dark.

My circumstances had changed, and I needed to accept it or be wrecked by it. Gradually, God taught me the beauty of allowing Him to fill in the gaps for my children.

When you can't change where you're at, allow God to bring grace into those empty spaces. Know this—your children will grow as they watch you grow and accept things you cannot change.

My daughters learned to cook so well they usually didn't need a recipe.

They learned to serve others with less expectation of being entertained.

My little buddy learned to knock out his chore list even when Mama wasn't around.

The things I wanted to protect my children from were being used to teach my children the very things they would need in the adult world.

When you accept things you can't change, you'll find courage to embrace your season and find good in it.

Every mother needs freedom from the voice in the back of her head telling her she's never enough. When you're walking with God and following His voice, *you are enough and you don't have to be everything.*

Allowing your soul to find peace even when you can't change things for your children brings you to a whole new level of dependence on God. This is where God moves. This is where He shows Himself. This is where your soul finds freedom from self-imposed expectations that have nothing to do with a mother "not being enough."

God is good.

He promises soul freedom.

He graces you with the ability to do all He's called you to do.

God doesn't pressure you, wear you out, or push you beyond your limitations. We do that to ourselves.

Every mother has enough hours in her day to do what she's called to do. Hear that, mothers—I didn't say we have enough hours to do the things we think we should do. *God knows our life, our story, our needs—and He tailor cuts His call on each of our days in accordance with what He sees we need to accomplish.*

It's OK if you don't have time to join the worship team anymore, volunteer at various places, or bake your child's birthday cake from scratch. I used to do all of the above, and more. But God calls me now to give my time to my children when I get home from work rather than to run off "feeling good" that I'm serving.

All we ever need to do is listen in to God. Trust Him to fill in the gaps you can't fill. That's all He ever wanted you to do.

Some of us are in places where we can no longer live the "perfect" mom life we tried to live for so long. ***Forced to let go of our ideal parenting style, we now need to trust God more than we ever trusted our method.*** Perhaps, sisters, this is where He wanted us all along.

The shame and blame game that plays itself in our heads even when we're doing our best is not the Father's heart for us. He gives peace.

Little Buddy loved his movie that night on my bed where I crashed so hard after a week's work. His sister asked me to hang out in her room while she painted, so I tucked him in, then joined her on her bed.

Trusting God with your time allows you to pull what you need from the moments He gives you. Trust Him, and live free.

Lord Jesus, thank You that the push and pull we feel is not from You. Help us respond to Your invitation to peace.

DAY 83

I have not come to call the righteous, but sinners to repentance. (Luke 5:32, ESV)

Today my growing child sat on my bed and talked. I listened, realizing how privileged I was as he shared one step of growth after another and how he had been promoted to leader in his group because of his good conduct and character.

There are few things as fun for a mama to hear, and I smiled as I showed the appreciation he was wanting not only from his group, but from his mother.

Then, I did an internal pause as I continued to scratch the back before me. (At our house, back scratches are a big deal.) I did a sober retake, because not all of mothering has been this golden. Truth be told, some of us mothers do our very best by our children, but end up walking them through things we never dreamed of.

God wants us to be a steadying factor in our children's lives rather than depend on them to steady us. He wants us to hold the course and stand on the solid rock of Jesus Christ in absolute dependence rather than fluctuate with our children as we watch them struggle and grow.

The struggle for growth often ends up producing the most growth.

The struggle to believe often produces stronger faith than if they had never doubted at all.

I can be as codependent on my children's performance as I can be on any other thing. God wants me dependent on Him. My peace is to be constant, rather than perfect one day when my son shares victory with me, then gone the next day when things are a struggle.

When our children struggle most, they need to see our peace most. As you turn the pages of this book, take heart to walk alongside your child and put your hand in Jesus's hand as you face giants and enter valleys where all you can do is cry out to the Lord for mercy and help.

I wonder how many of us moms feel that utter dependence daily, and how many of us are able to tap into peace.

I see us moms fighting valiantly for our children while missing out on peace. The accusations come long and hard, overriding the gentle invitation of our Father who invites us to rest even as we do the hardest thing we will ever do.

"Your kitchen is still dirty. What have you been doing all day?"

"Your garden is full of weeds. What must the neighbors think of your family?"

"You came home too late for Bible stories. How will your child feel well-loved tonight?"

"You let your child go to that outing. What if something happens and it's all your fault?"

"You made your child stay home because you didn't have peace about the place or people. What if he rebels and feels stifled?"

The onslaught on our minds can be enough to have us in a constant state of tension, entirely missing out on the very things that will most draw our children to Christ—peace and joy.

Satan loves this. He takes our passionate love and uses it to produce panic.

God does the opposite. Always, always, always, He invites His daughters to peace.

Fear-based parenting is unheard of in God's vocabulary.

Just yesterday I sat with a group of moms, watching our children fish in the cool evening air while we laughed along with them and served them snacks. Fish and turtles were caught, delighted over, and splashed right back into the pond.

In that moment, I realized that the simplest things of motherhood for our children can be the largest acts of worship to our God.

The universe spins a little more smoothly when all us mothers accept the invitation to peace.

My child may be sitting on my bed chatting with me about his life today. Tomorrow, he may struggle to bite his tongue or obey. If I am unacquainted with peace, I'll lose it one day and have superficial peace the next day, all depending on how well my children respond.

This is not God's heart for me or for you.

Jesus Christ is our solid rock and He calls us to be an anchor when our children don't know how to steady themselves.

Mothers, as you read the pages of this book, know this: the best of the best of you may still have children who struggle long and hard. This can push you to panic, but if you allow Jesus to enter your soul, it will invite you to peace instead.

In that peace you will find Jesus as you've never found Him before.

His mercy is outstanding and His grace incomprehensible, while His wisdom surpasses anything you could conjure up on your own.

All is grace, and may you feel it in your bones and marrow—this overwhelming peace that passes understanding, that will keep you steady, that will allow you to be a haven for each child during seasons of struggle and growth.

Father, thank You for coming to this earth for needy people. Thank You for walking with us more closely than ever when we walk with our children through rough patches of their lives. Thank You for everlasting hope and peace.

DAY 84

The Lord will keep you from evil; He will keep your life. The Lord will keep your going out and your coming in from this time forth and forever more. (Psalm 121:7–8, ESV)

Every once in a while, the word "mother" hits me with force—like when I woke this morning realizing I had to take the cat in for surgery and she wasn't supposed to have breakfast, but Little Buddy was almost certainly downstairs feeding his beloved Cassie.

I flew out of bed, opened the garage door (where she sleeps because I refuse to have litter boxes in the house), and sure enough, there was the fifth "child" of the family happily chowing down her food.

I removed the food hastily, washed my hair, plopped the cat in a laundry basket and covered it with a swimming towel, hoping she wouldn't jump out. Then I ran out the door without my coffee, makeup, or brushed hair.

I looked and felt like a real scarecrow.

And since I was new in town I needed that beloved GPS voice talking to me the whole way, telling me where to go for this low-cost spay and neuter place. Even with that, I looped the roundabout twice before I pulled into the parking lot and walked in the door.

No mom should ever have to stress about cats at 6:45 a.m. Just saying.

The room was full of yowling cats, mournfully awaiting surgery—and I stared in amazement at these happy women who chose to work there. They stared back at me and dully informed me that my cat couldn't leave the place in a laundry basket, then dumped an extra $8 on my bill for a cardboard carrier.

I had even told them that we did indeed have a cat carrier, but it was borrowed and had not been returned. I think they believed me, the crazy-haired woman who was so obviously not a cat person.

The real cat girl in this family is my thirteen-year-old. Because I love her, I "love" her cat. Because her uncles love her, they also "love" her cat, agreeing to haul it from the West Coast to the East, caring for it as they went. One uncle even tried walking it on a leash. *Now that's dedication*, but to the girl more than to the cat.

Life is never perfect. From cats to kids, if a mother can accept that one thing, many pounds of stress will roll right off her back.

Most things just aren't a big deal, mothers. There are a million reasons to stress but there's one very great reason *not to*. The simple truth is that God wants a whole army of mothers who live in peace and accept their own bits of daily fragmentation with grace.

A few days prior to surgery day for the cat, I'd driven this same child somewhere but had snapped at her in the car. It came out of nowhere and I was shocked with myself. I'd been carrying stress and it shot out at one of the people I loved. Since children are full of grace, they forgive easily after a sincere apology—but I hated myself for what I'd done.

"I was so wrong. I was such a bad parent just now. I'm so sorry." I must have said those words a hundred times—and by the end of the day she must have reached out to give a hundred hugs and kisses to her mama who always wanted to bring healing but had ended up hurting her, instead.

But, my imperfection at that moment allowed me to show her repentance.

My imperfection allowed her to give the perfect gift of forgiveness.

My imperfection allowed both of us to live out the heart of God when He asks sin to be acknowledged and tossed aside for better things, while the offended one gives grace just like He did.

I want to encourage us mothers not to accept our sin, but to accept grace when we sin.

I want us to transfer that peace into every area of our lives where there are a million reasons, every day, to stress—but most of them are simply not worth the energy.

Rather than waste energy, we need to transfer our energy to good things. When we're taken with stress over minor things we leave little room to bless with larger things.

Let it roll off your back, Mama. Stop yourself. Breathe. Then smile and say something kind rather than critical or stressful.

Stop complaining and start thanking.

Back to the cat. She has been such a good part of my daughter's life and entirely worth the effort. Even so, there have been a hundred reasons to stress over that feline.

It cost plenty just to move her into this rental house with us.

She got fleas.

She kept running out the door and getting pregnant.

She needed surgery after litter *nine.*

She pooped on the bathroom floor the other night when someone left her in the house for too long.

When she wants to, she drinks out of the toilet until someone spots her and hastily removes her. (*Gross with a capital G.*)

She slobbers on the couch.

With each litter of kittens, we advertise and meet with strangers until they all have homes and I breathe a sigh of relief even as my daughter's chocolate eyes fill with tears over sad good-byes.

If I allow the negative to make me chuck the cat right out the door, I'll deprive my daughter of this wonderful experience of bonding with a pet and doing what it takes to care for it.

I'll deprive her of raising money from those nine litters so she could buy her own iPhone. (Yes, that happened.)

I'll deprive all my children (and their friends) from snuggling furry little creatures in the morning when they wake up.

In the same way, mothers, we deprive ourselves of one large, beautiful life when we stress over a million little things.

Let's learn to focus, channel our energy, let go, live free, and laugh a little.

Then, speak out one of your thousand gifts and mention it to your children. Your life will change—I promise—and so will theirs!

Father, thank You for offering us perfect love in an imperfect world. Help us to look for perfection in areas that liberate us rather than bind us up.

Day 85

Behold, I have graven you on the palms of my hands; your walls are continually before me. (Isaiah 49:16, ESV)

She's sitting there, and her lower lip trembles.

She's letting it all out. For many years she has performed in order to gain or keep approval and love—and it didn't work. In fact, she got yuck when she tried so hard for love.

The tears won't stop, and they pour hot and long. I say it as firmly to her as I've said it to myself: "You are not loved because you dress well, accomplish a lot, or because you love your kids. You can just be who you are—and be *valued, treasured, and worth a lot.*"

She sits, silent, absorbing the words. For someone who's worked her entire life—worked for God, parents, husband, and kids—with little thought or focus on her own ease, these words are a gold mine.

She's not a selfish person; she's a giver. And she needs to hear it—*her worth is not based on what she does or how perfect she is.*

When you criticize your children for every little failure, you have a recipe for a hardworking performer who will eventually crash and burn.

Our value is based on the Son of God and His thoughts of us. It is based on the fact that we were created in His image and He wanted us. Hear this—*you can work your entire life to gain approval without knowing how much you were approved before you ever did a thing.*

Outward actions do matter, but they must be the fruit of a heart that's already approved by God, not the striving of a heart seeking approval from God and man.

When we know how much we're already loved by God, we enter rest. In this rest, we show love best to those around us. We *want* to get up and serve others. We truly desire to give, and give well. We sacrifice.

All of it becomes a circle of love rather than a striving for love. Circles go round and round with no end of exhaustion, because you receive love from God as you give out love to His people. Here, we also learn not to expect perfect love from imperfect humans, but to know and receive perfect love from a perfect God.

If your lips are trembling today, remember who you were when you were born, and how much you were loved and adored by God—and most likely, everyone in the room who laid eyes on your wet, sticky, helpless little body. You are the same human being today—loved before performance. Resting in that will enable you to live well.

Remember to *be* in a state of love before you try to give out love. If we can learn this ourselves and teach it to our children, we will have accomplished much.

Father, thank You so much that You don't love us based on our performance. Thank You that Your love brings us to peace, and that peace allows us to do Your will from a place of rest and belonging. Help us offer the same security to our children.

Day 86

I am the vine, you are the branches. Whoever abides in me and I in him,
he it is who bears much fruit. For apart from me you can do nothing.
(John 15:5, ESV)

The alarm buzzed much too early, and I swung my feet onto the
floor with a prayer.

"God, anoint this day. Anoint me today."

When you grip a microphone to help lead worship for several hundred people, somehow all your faults come marching through your brain—and it feels as if they're in plain sight of everyone before you.

I hate hypocrisy. One of my favorite postures before the Lord is one of repentance, because I know what I am without Him, and how much I fail my God and those around me. Repentance is a gift given to me by God, this merciful God who doesn't render out what we all deserve—and even turns around and uses us to propel His name forward.

We had just moved, and I spun about life as one of those mortally wounded flies gasping for one last breath before giving up—and in the process, I lost out on that tender peace and Presence that comes when we pause and soak it all in.

Moving, then acquiring a semitruck load of wood to cut up as quickly as possible, then watching the garden grow up in weeds because the friend you garden with is also moving—well, I rather lived as though there was no tomorrow and it all needed to be done yesterday.

I missed sitting at His feet, soaking up His love. And I was beyond excited to have an entire morning at church doing just that with some of my dearly loved fellow worshipers who love Jesus, and who I get to watch, lean in on their lives, and glean from them.

It's glorious to sing out truth and proclaim Jesus. Even practice can become a worship time, and we all pause in wonder at the glory-presence in the room with us.

He says He's with us—*all the time.* Just because we don't feel His presence all the time doesn't mean He's not with us all the time. But when we don't abide in Him, we become an empty vessel with no sound.

The mic gave out on me suddenly that day, becoming a cold, dead weight in my hand. I bumped my voice into it, but no sound. It was like a dead body—heavy, cold, and lifeless. Once new batteries were put in, my voice became clear as the instrument channeled it correctly and propelled it out.

When our hearts aren't abiding in Christ, when we lose out on the Presence and cease to host it well, we become a bit like the microphone did that day—dead, cold, and heavy. Christ is our battery, our life force, our propeller for those around us.

When we host Him, we host life, we give life, we encourage those around us, and we bring light wherever we go. We become a magnet for grace, and we draw others right to its source.

The world craves love and watches for joy. It doesn't need more preachers stepping behind the pulpit trying to build their own little empires while they deny Jesus access. The world is waiting, watching, and longing for the authentic and real.

The real is felt more than it is spoken.

Real life draws, pulls, and sheds light over the greatest darkness. Real life must be claimed in the heart before it can be proclaimed to the world—or to our children.

You can name it, or you can truly claim it. As the microphone brings forth greater sound and beauty than we could ever do on our own, so Christ brings great life to your otherwise merely human existence.

If you name the name of Christ, keep your batteries charged and make Christ your propeller into all things lovely. Allow your children to live in an atmosphere of *grace.*

Lord Jesus, we were made to crave so much more than our own existence. Thank You for creating us with longing that can only be satisfied in total abandonment and worship to You.

DAY 87

Charge them that are rich in this world, that they be not high minded nor trust in uncertain riches, but in the living God, Who gives us richly all things to enjoy. (1 Timothy 6:17, ESV)

The old red barn leaned to one side, but I was charmed.

My earliest memories included barns. I loved listening to my father sing while he milked his cows, and I'd stare into rafters, fascinated with the heights, while pigeons fluttered around and cooed softly.

In my father's barn, I followed hens and chicks as closely as they allowed me to, owned my very first pig, and found freshly born foals wobbling beside their mamas. I skated down the aisles on roller skates and watched my older sisters learn how to clean a cow's udder before milking.

Barns are still my favorite. And this one—the old, red, leaning barn—was prepared to host a dance.

Lights hung from high rafters while a rustic chandelier graced the center of the lofty, vaulted roof. The floor was swept bare while hay bales stood on the side for folks to sit and watch the dancers.

The dance was for someone else's family reunion, and my girls were green with envy, as was I. Who doesn't want a good old barn dance?

I had promoted healthy, clean dancing to the girls because I wanted them exposed to wholesome fun before they had a chance to be lured by sensual club atmospheres. I spoke with them about all of our inborn need and desire for fun, and how Christians need it just as much as anyone.

God created fun, laughter, and joy. Living with the false idea that having fun is not "spiritual" only leads you away from the Spirit. Living in legalism opens our soul to a greater desire for wrong.

Promoting God and good is our greatest weapon against evil. Allowing the good in our lives gives us less room and desire for the bad.

Promoting good is just as important as renouncing evil. As in the case with dancing and daughters, promoting their joy when they are young may keep them from less desirable things when they reach adolescence. But keeping them on a taught string of "holiness" and no fun while constantly preaching against evil may strengthen the propensity for evil in their hearts.

If your life is drab and joyless, take a look. In the name of God, are you being led toward the things of God? Are you bringing love and joy?

When we dub God's gifts as worldly, we lose out on one of the greatest attributes of God. He loves to watch us enjoy life. *God is a life-giver, not a joy-drainer.*

If you pursue something you love and it does create more cause for temptation, perhaps you need to let it go. Pursue Christ, walk purely, and love Him above all else. Find another outlet that you can enjoy. But make sure you find one when you let go of another.

Some of my friends don't take one sip of wine because they know that one sip will lead to many drinks. Others can enjoy a glass of wine daily and it causes no problem. Only you can know which thing is your downfall and which can stay in a wholesome place.

Counterfeit "holiness" based on legalism is one of the surest causes of death. Satan is always out to convince our hearts that good things are wrong and wrong things are good. One can be as detrimental as the other, for we are human beings in a natural body, created purposefully to enjoy certain things.

Joy is a gift. Anything wholesome that brings joy is a gift. Just as we delight in happy kids, so God delights in us enjoying His gifts. As a mother, receive His gifts into your life and make the most of them!

Last Sunday our worship pastor laid hands on our ten-year-old daughter, the one who said she wanted to come to church early with me because she felt God move in a special way. I had exposed her on purpose to the goodness of God as He moves among His people because I wanted her to see the reality of my words.

"I don't need anything bad for a boost in my spirit," I told the kids. "God gives me so much joy when I worship Him."

She went, and she saw. She felt, and she heard. And when the worship pastor prayed over her, she received his words gladly. "God gave you the desire for the things you love," he told her.

She had asked me about those things earlier, and as he prayed, the pastor felt impressed with dance for my daughter. Perhaps she would worship through her dance, and he encouraged me to talk with her about closing her bedroom door, turning on music, and dancing for the Lord.

I found her the next night and walked the yard with her. "Mother, don't you know I already do that? I write songs to Jesus, then I dance to them."

At ten years old, she's found a creative, fun outlet. At fifteen, I hope we find even more. Perhaps there will be square dancing and fun trips to concerts. There will be more ballet lessons if she still desires them. There will be wholesome parties and many opportunities for fun.

In the name of God, are we being led toward the things of God? Are we exuding joy?

My friends who hosted the reunion and barn dance said they hadn't had a fun weekend like that in a long time. They are hardworking, homeschooling, Jesus-loving people—but it still remains that they are human and in need of enjoyment.

So are you! God created you for it—and He wants you to promote His goodness more than you proclaim Satan's evil. As you fill your life and your kids' lives with goodness, hearts will be full and there will be less desire for evil than if you sit in the dust declaring everything wrong.

Whatever your "red barn" is, find it!

Father, thank You for providing us with so many good things to enjoy. Help us never portray You as the stealer of joy, but as the giver of it.

Day 88

Rejoice with those who rejoice, weep with those who weep. (Romans 12:15, ESV)

I smiled as I walked into my kitchen and watched her wipe my countertops to a sheen.

Every dish was thoroughly rinsed and nearly clean before she even placed it into the dishwasher. And this morning she was at it before her coffee or shower was over. My kitchen had never seen a guest like this before.

She taught me how to perfect my coffee, how to create nutritious drinks as delicious as ones you can get at Starbucks. Plates were filled artistically, colorfully, and carefully. And my family soon grew to love her cooking while I urged her to create her own cookbook.

When I wake, on the other hand, the kitchen is the last place I want to be. I'm thinking of that painting project or yard cleanup, the writing inspiration, or getting laundry started. I'll leave dishes for the kids to do, and quickly stir up a pot of oats for breakfast just because our bodies force us to think about food.

Many days I'm gulping bites down quickly while I'm running around the kitchen. Preparing meals must be done, but truth be told, it's not what I'd love to focus on.

We laugh about it together. We'd make great roommates because we balance each other perfectly. I'd keep the house and yard spotless and she'd keep everyone fed and the kitchen clean.

I was tempted to compare myself with her, especially when the kids raved over her meals while I let the fridge run emptier, cooking simple meals speedily so I'd have time to settle into our new home. But the beauty of it all was, *we balanced each other*, and when I really thought about it, I was content to be me.

Sara, who loves outdoor chores and summer nights, carrying pallets over her head to a bonfire.

Sara, who cooks large pots of food in a matter of minutes, then runs away and out to do other things.

Sara, who wakes in the morning excited to run outside before the world stirs.

I'm just me, plain and simple. And every day there are opportunities for comparison or contentment.

This morning I caught myself again. I was sitting in the back of the church, observing other girls' hair and clothing. How can some people be *that beautiful*? Effortless class and radiant beauty always strikes me.

God nudged me as quickly as comparison thoughts judged me.

"Sara, jealousy is no longer a part of who you are. You are loved, safe, and held. You are OK."

Breathe. It's OK to breathe your own air.

Just yesterday someone had criticized me for what seemed like the hundredth time. This person seemed to love "fixing" me, no matter what I did or said, and the last words got to me as I doubled over in that inward fetal position of self-protection.

Somewhere along the way, I had gotten hurt and had spent many years feeling less than good enough. I found myself nervous, weighing words before I spoke them, cringing in wait for the next someone to notice where I went wrong. It was emotionally debilitating.

God began to show me that He had a word to speak over me. That before my visible questions of identity formed, He had His own unwavering statements about me while He formed me invisibly in my mother's womb.

Rather than find myself, I needed to find what God said about Himself and His thoughts and His creation—because I was part of what He made.

He showed me that my own hurts were not an excuse for insecurity or comparison, and that I was responsible for whether or not I continued to listen in on self-hatred.

I was responsible. I had to choose. I had to take hold of life before death grabbed me once again.

I turned around at church today and introduced myself to the prettiest girl there, with the loveliest family. Good grief, how can every single member of her family be that gorgeous?

I relax, and I smile. I reach into lives and hearts, then I do it again, and again, and again. It doesn't matter who is outwardly perfect or who is less beautiful. I look into souls as I want them to look into mine.

Here, I find complete peace, and here, I am content.

Here, I get to home in on what God's placed in my heart to do. I get to enjoy it, thrill over it, and cultivate it. Because God creates us purposefully to do the things He wants accomplished on this earth, and all we need to do is what we do best.

In heaven, there's a multitude of angels praising the one savior.

There's a heavenly host with no thought but to worship the creator of the universe.

But long ago, there was one who coveted the place of God and desired to be like God. Cast down from the heavenlies, he now waits about God's creation, trying to convince us that we, too, should have more glory, more power, more attention.

But life is not so much about seeking to be noticed as it is about noticing and seeking God. When we seek the face of God, we are rewarded with the things of God, the heart of the Father, the passion He breathes into us that keeps us from apathy and dull living.

All the things of God come from gazing into the face of God, and you don't need to wow people with anything; you just need to live Christ in everything.

When you give up your natural tendency of comparison, God gives you a place of grace not to be compared or replaced by anything better. Whatever things you consider gain to yourself, you must cast them down so that Christ be replaced by nothing.

As Michael Tait says, "We are not called because we're talented; we are talented because we are called."

See this: You are not loved or wanted because you're good at something; you are loved and wanted because God is good at everything, and He created you, a good thing. He has business to accomplish, and He equips His people to accomplish it.

Reach out your hand, and share your heart. Be glad in the face of all beauty, for God loves His creation. Relax, and smile—others will be drawn to you as they see in you what they know to be true.

My friend and I love each other so dearly there is no room for jealousy. She's happy that I know how to decorate well, and I'm happy she loves to cook. If she ever creates her own cookbook, I will be her greatest cheerleader.

I want to be everyone's cheerleader. All good comes from God and calls for cheering on. Let the fallen angels remain in their state—as for me, I shall join the ranks around the throne who want nothing but to worship God and rejoice in all His goodness.

Father, thank You that because of You, all goodness leads us to You. You created it and it can make us happy whether it's our own blessing or another mother's blessing. Help us be free of comparison and simply rejoice.

DAY 89

But God chose what is foolish in the world to shame the wise; God chose what is weak in the world to shame the strong; God chose what is low and despised in the world, even things that are not, to bring to nothing things that are, so that no human being might boast in the presence of God.

And because of Him you are in Christ Jesus, who became to us wisdom from God, righteousness and sanctification and redemption, so that, as it is written, 'Let the one who boasts, boast in the LORD.'" (1 Corinthians 1:27–31, ESV)

"Mom, come look at this," she requested.

I looked at her TikTok for the hundredth time and smiled at an elderly grandpa who was filming himself.

It made my daughter happy, this child who'd left her friends and moved to the other side of the country. I smiled with her and turned back to making omelets stuffed with all things wonderful and healthy . . . until bacon topped it all off.

But wait—bacon's healthy, too—right?

I've known people to eat bacon even when they chuck sugar and almost every carb the universe owns. "Bacon is protein," they say. I nod my head and agree because I love the stuff.

When it comes to methods, there are few things as controversial as diet. And rightly so as we watch our country blow up in obesity while inhaling large sodas and fries, Pop-Tarts, and deep-fried Oreos (don't ask if I ever tried one). The cancer rate skyrockets, and families mourn the loss of loved ones.

Just last night I took my daughter out to use her Starbucks gift card, and there were 569 calories in her grande Oreo chocolate Frappuccino. I thought to myself, "*I will never drink one of those.*" But who knows? I might!

There are many things we mothers purpose to never, ever do. I was the stay-at-home, homeschool mom driving an old minivan so I could afford to be home with my children. I gave them green smoothies to drink and cooked oatmeal to eat. I wanted them to be healthy and happy, and I believed that started with a good diet.

Then life hit, and it hit hard. When circumstances forced me to go to work, all my children went to public school. When my situation got even worse, I gathered my four together and made a massive move from the West Coast to the East Coast.

I learned to trust God when I had to do things I never thought I'd do. I learned to make changes and breathe through them. I learned to be more flexible in what I said I'd never do.

I've seen many mothers say "I will *never . . .*" yet continue each day in frustration and exhaustion while her children struggle under the weight of a joyless atmosphere. I'm here to encourage all of us to be open to adjusting our expectations.

It's easy for all of us to keep doing what we've always done even when it's not really working the best for our children. Maybe you'll never be forced to pick up and move cross country, but in any circumstance, it's easy to get stuck in our own expectations and lose sight of changes God may be wanting us to make.

When COVID-19 hit us hard right after moving, I lowered my expectations and allowed the children to sleep later, have more screen time, etc. We baked and ate plenty of dessert, sometimes just because we needed something creative to do to keep from going nuts. I needed to adjust what I expected of them so they could get through this time. It wasn't a forever season even when it felt like it.

Mothers, what adjustments might God be prompting you to make so you can bring more life and joy to your children? Remember that the end of all things is love. Is your child finding love and peace in your standards of what should and shouldn't be?

My daughter resumed her TikTok while I kept making omelets just because I could and I didn't need to head out the door for work that day. We both smiled. Sometimes God uses unexpected things in unexpected ways. And sometimes He wants to remove our methods so we learn to improve, alter, or change what we're doing. When the methods we use to implement goodness end up bringing more stress or tension, we may need to change to a plan we didn't think was as good—but that will end up bringing the greatest good.

Mothers, may we learn to trust the Master more than our own method. Follow His voice, and be open to change!

Lord Jesus, You are so good at removing our props so You can be our pillar. Thank You for always pulling us back to this place of dependence and worship.

DAY 90

I am the Vine; you are the branches. Whoever abides in me and I in him,
he it is that bears much fruit, for apart from Me you can do nothing.
(John 15:5, ESV)

I looked at him and said bluntly, "I want what you have."

Some people are a magnet for grace. This friend—well, one look at his face across the room let me know he was one of those God-people.

He didn't just talk about it—he owned Jesus and Jesus owned him. And God did breathtaking things through him because God was in him.

When God is within you, big things happen because He's a big God. There's no room for apathy because God is doing exciting things in you, through you, for you. Others are drawn to your source because each human heart craves a source greater than their own.

In this technology-savvy world where people get to promote themselves to thousands with the push of a single button, where they get to hold selfie sticks out far enough to capture themselves, where they are taught to compete more than serve, and feel pressure to acquire personal followers more than they are led to follow the one who created each person—in this world, *one must be intent on knowing Jesus, because it won't just happen.*

He drew me in long ago. But there was this *stuff* I kept carrying, and I was always captivated when I met someone with clarity and joy

I wanted more than to warm another church pew. If God was real and good, satisfying and magnificent, why were so many churches dead enough to turn souls away more than draw them? Why do 75 percent of youth leave rather than cleave? Why did I dread another stuffy sermon but light up with joy when the real and authentic stood to speak *only for the promotion of Jesus Christ*?

You can rather feel it in the air when someone has an additional agenda. Tacked right up there with knowing Jesus is the interest in their own promotion. This brings a sickening vibe into their person and makes them create club-based operations called "church," be offended when people leave "their" church, and preach what it takes to keep people there rather than live out Jesus so real that it draws people to Him.

Replacing Jesus with a mere knowledge of the Bible shrivels up the very foundation on which Christianity was birthed. To be a Christian means to be a "little Christ."

It doesn't mean growing up with Christian parents.

It doesn't mean going to church (though being with God's people is vital).

It doesn't mean marrying a good person and starting the good family all over again.

Being a Christian means knowing Jesus so fully that He becomes a part of yourself. Without knowing it, you become a magnet for people like my friend is, because people are created to crave this source of life.

I watched young and old, male and female, pursue his presence. I watched faces light up—because he was lit up. And though I knew his time was entirely booked, I asked for ten minutes for myself. He gave it gladly—only he gave an hour.

Christ is a giver. When others are in your presence, do they sense you giving out rays of light, encouragement, and joy? Do they know you are interested in them because you love them?

Mothers, more than to anyone else, this is our call to our children. This is our mandate from heaven.

Your actions are merely a symptom of what's inside. Therefore, trying to remedy your actions will prove futile and fruitless. You must host Christ and ask Him to take over from the inside out.

Our sinful nature will never, ever change on our own. We may grit our teeth in determination, but unless Christ abides in us we are taken with our own agenda. Even loving on others can become selfish because we want our agenda of "being a good person."

But when Christ has His place in your heart, He loves others right through you because He is love. You don't realize how much you're drawing others because you're just being you.

No striving to be something or someone. Simply loving Christ and enjoying His presence.

This, mothers, is the one and only way to be a true Christian. Allow Him to take you where He wants to bring you—you, ***created as one to whom all His promises are meant to flow.***

You will be as my friend is—a magnet for the grace of God and His favor all over your life.

Father, thank You that it's all about You. Thank You for removing the weight from our shoulders and allowing us to look away from ourselves to a good and glorious God who never fails.

Day 91

Do not be anxious about anything, but in everything by prayer and supplication with thanksgiving let your requests be made known to God. And the peace of God, which surpasses all understanding, will guard your hearts and your minds in Christ Jesus. (Philippians 4:6–7, ESV)

I'm painting today, that old KILZ stuff that drips everywhere because it's runny—not to mention it doesn't clean up well because its oil-based.

It's hot outside, and the older kids are off to Walmart after a busy morning of stacking wood with their friends.

Strong bodies are needed for stacking wood. I appreciate each lifted piece—until the tones lift along with the wood, and there's some sass in the mix.

There's been more sassy faces and tones in my house than I'd like to admit. The kids are all getting older and suddenly, they all have opinions. Life isn't as simple as handing them each a cookie and a garden hose to fill a huge tub of water on a hot day.

I try to drench their hot little attitudes with lectures just like the tot I'm babysitting drenches her feet with a cold stream of water—but sometimes, my lectures only turn their hot tones into cold vibes.

I want warm. I want warmth *all the time* from these four little people I've given birth to. And if anything makes me prone to worry, it's failing these little big people.

Just the other day, my mouth dropped open when my daughter and I stood before the mirror and she was taller than I. We'd been waiting for this day and now it's here.

I'm worried. The handsome dude who likes her, the look on her face as she struggles to accommodate life as it's given her, and the legs growing taller, constantly in need of new jeans to accommodate the growth.

But Jesus asks me not to worry. He asks me to walk close to His heart and love Him extravagantly.

Like Mary, He asks me to wash His feet. I bow before Him in the early morning, when all is still except for the youngest early bird spooning peanut butter into his oatmeal and playing with the dog while he waits for Mama to stir.

Because when I simply storm through life day after day after day, I get dryer than these British Columbia forests set ablaze and sending their smoky haze over the sea to Washington State.

We live under the smoky haze these days—and when we worry we live under a haze worse than smoke because the eyes of our hearts are dimmed to peace, love, and joy.

Worry robs us of the very things we want our kids to be most drawn to.

We worry about how to fix this or that, and end up facedown—because worry consumes our hearts, and God can't fill a heart that's already full of something else.

He comes in the knowing. Our war strategy is one of learning what it means to host His presence and know Him as savior God and greatest friend. ***Our war is fought in our worship—because worship replaces worry and grants us access right into the throne room of God where He receives our sacrifice of praise.***

We need to drop our worry even if we're worried for a good cause.

Get this, mothers—you can know God so intimately that your kids can sense Him in the room when you pray over their beds at night.

You can pray for your kids with utterances only God knows. You can worship Him as your kids wake, and allow them to walk into your sacred place where they will see a glimpse of it before the day begins.

You can turn on the TV screen but turn it on to worship music to serenade their morning routine.

You can guide them to read the Bible and pray each day, encouraging them to really seek the face of God while they're young.

You can hold their faces at night and ask heaven to come down and touch them as they sleep.

See this, mama who is worried sick about growing kids—you can do and be so much good for your kids, but you must do it without worry, because worry dims the light you want them to see.

Worry holds onto the finite when God asks us to trust His infinity.

Worry is selfish because it replaces God.

When you refuse to worry, you allow the joy-gates to swing open, and you will begin to wonder why you haven't lived in this free zone for much longer.

Worry must be dropped in order for God's work to be picked up. You cannot hold both.

Worry infuses you with fear; worship releases the God-presence into your being. *Kids need the God flavor more than they need the mother worry.*

Because God does things mother can never do, and mother needs to allow God to live His presence right in her, so He can do for her what He does so well.

Just the other week, my son pitched a fit of distress at the end of a long day. I asked him to come over to me on the lawn, lay on my chest, and just stop. He fell asleep with no more cares.

God asks us to come. You will never be enough, ever—but that's why you have a God who is always enough, always. Simply host Him in your bones and marrow, and you will see His hand all over your life.

KILZ is drying on old bathroom walls, and I still need to decide on a consequence for the child who knows one is coming. Tomorrow will be a new opportunity for me to worry about that, and getting that bathroom done, and whether or not I'm neglecting anything or anyone more important.

I'll be worrying about how to get things done, and then I'll worry that I'm doing *too* much and not caring for others like I want to.

But there's another way. I can learn that worry is futile, draw near to a God who holds the universe, and simply lean into Him and live out the best and good, as He wants to live it in me.

Because God holds my child, and He holds me—in fact, He holds the universe He created *entirely on His own.* (2 Chronicles 20:12)

Father, thank You that at the end of each day I can hand all my worries over to You, trusting You to show me which path to take and how to navigate each circumstance with my children. Thank You that I am Your child and You care for all of us even more than I care for my children.

DAY 92

You shall therefore lay up these words of mine in your heart and in your soul, and you shall bind them as a sign on your hand, and they shall be as frontlets between your eyes.

You shall teach them to your children, talking of them when you are sitting in your house, and when you are walking by the way, and when you lie down, and when you rise.

You shall write them on the doorposts of your house, and on your gates.

That your days and the days of your children may be multiplied in the land . . ." (Deuteronomy 11:18–21a, ESV)

I love driving in the car with all four kids, talking to them randomly about all that really matters. I love sitting with them at night, reading and discussing scripture. I love moments in the day that lead to opportunity to bring up a God principle and how to live it, here and now.

Surround your children with the Word more than with the world.

I love talking with them about the difference between religion and relationship; how one leads to hypocritical living and one to joy and passion. I love explaining to them how walking into a church building doesn't make them a Christian any more than standing in a garage makes them a car.

When we have Christ alive in our own hearts, this command to teach our kids when we sit, and rise, and walk will happen naturally.

Just as your body craves food when it's hungry, so your soul, when it's full of Jesus, will crave sharing Jesus with your children.

As Jesus said in Luke 19:40, "I tell you, if these were silent, the very stones would cry out."

And as Andrew Pudewa says, "The idea is, saturate the environment with what you want your children to internalize" (IEW, Institute for Excellence in Writing).

He speaks of violin teachers who surround the child with posters of musical notes and begin teaching them at very early ages. Of writing teachers who saturate the environment with words and ideas.

None of us need reminders of how communism is brainwashed into the minds of children, or of how people break down emotionally with constant criticism. What we hear affects our hearts. What we sense affects our spirits.

The good news is that children are also affected by good in the atmosphere, and it is up to us to surround them with it.

Mothers, our kids can sense, see, and feel what we are taken with. They will most likely be taken with the same. We release an atmosphere into their world all the time, and either it's barren, or it engages their soul and draws them in.

Feed them religion, and they will resent it.

Feed them joyful passion for Jesus, and they will be subconsciously drawn to the same thing you have even if they go through seasons of rebellion or doubt.

When I think of mothers I want to emulate, I think of Mary, Hannah, and Eunice.

Hannah was barren, and as she wept to the Lord for a child, she promised to give him right back to the Lord for service in the temple with the priest.

I'm not so sure I could have done what she did. But by age three, Samuel was ministering before Eli the priest. Hannah's fervent prayers granted her a son, and her dedication granted her one of the most godly men in history.

Mary was a simple girl from a small town, unmarried and knowing full well how her friends would perceive her if what the angel spoke came to pass. Yet, she immediately replied, "Behold, I am the servant of the Lord. Let it be to me according to your word" (Luke 1:38 ESV).

She put her love for the Lord above and beyond her desire for approval from her friends and fiancé. Joseph, when he discovered she was pregnant, was going to put her away privately. Imagine the pain of shame she must have felt even though she knew her innocence.

But she remained steadfast and, out of her purity of spirit, Christ Jesus came to earth.

Eunice's husband was a gentile and not a believer in Christ (Acts 16:1). I wonder if Eunice often prayed for her son Timothy to believe in spite of his father's doubt. We see Timothy loving Jesus and growing beyond most men his age. He became like a son to the Apostle Paul, who urged him to be an example of godliness, faith, and holiness so that no one would despise his youth.

Eunice's mother Lois was also a believer. How encouraging to see a heritage of believers affecting a son even though his father was an unbeliever!

Take heart, those of you who wonder how your children will learn to love the Lord with an unsaved father. If you walk in the Spirit, God's Spirit will be felt, seen, and heard through you. Walk purely, in honor and respect toward your husband so the Word of God is not blasphemed. However wearying your life has become, you hold in your hands an awesome opportunity.

Lord Jesus, You are Spirit, and those who worship You must worship in spirit and truth. Thank You that You're alive and want to bring life through my heart to my children's hearts. Thank You that You are more than words and head knowledge—You are seen and felt with the joy of relationship.

Day 93

Give, and it will be given to you. Good measure, pressed down, shaken together, running over, will be put into your lap. (Luke 6:38, ESV)

I was on jury duty as I sat in the back row of the county courthouse and listened in as a few prisoners pleaded their case to the black-robed judge.

Self-pitying, victimizing words rose through the room rather than apology and desire to become a better citizen. One young man basically was blaming the law because now, after being in jail, "he literally has nothing." I wondered if his parents handed him everything in life and he never learned to deny himself and be a contributor.

Another young man walked behind the table and sat down with words much different. Regret, responsibility, and genuine words of how he would repay the system were on his lips. I wondered, again, who his parents were and how they taught him.

A few weeks later I was stranded in a strawberry field with bowls of picked berries and four dusty kids. I summoned enough courage to ask a stranger if he had jumper cables to restart my dead battery.

He looked at me and told me he has two buckets of berries to pick and will finish filling the first bucket and then help me out. I explained that I have kids and berries waiting in the car, and that I would just call a friend. He went back to filling his bucket with berries and again told me how much he has to do.

I walked back to the car and explained to the kids what had just happened. I explained what our friend, who was on his way to help us, will do. They saw the difference. One man went out of his way to help, another went out of his way not to help.

Earlier in the berry patch I had a lazy kid. I told him that if he will not help he will get no strawberry shortcake. I meant every word and he bent his back over the row again.

Laziness is inherent in most of us. A mother is responsible to train her children to serve willingly. *This happens in the course of daily life as we teach them to pitch in with whatever is going on.*

Children need to be contributing members in your household. At two and three they can help unload the dishwasher and set the table.

A few years later they can learn to dust furniture well.

A few years later they can scrub the bathroom.

Have a small garden where you teach them to care for plants and pull weeds.

At our house, I don't do allowances. I explain to the kids that Mommy doesn't get paid for doing laundry, and we all help out because we all make work. The kids make money by doing outside jobs or when I pay them for something we both agree on.

This is creating kids who are eager for jobs. They know that in order to have money, they need to work hard.

The older kids jump on weeding opportunities for the neighbor or offer to do extra, more difficult chores for me when they want to make money. I love watching them head happily to the neighbor's house for a weeding job because they are excited about making money.

My son begs to work for the neighbors because he's saving up for something he wants, expensive shoes that I won't buy for him. If he pays half, I pay the rest.

I love watching him run into the house with a wad of cash, jubilant over his success. He's happier working hard than many kids are lounging around in front of the TV with allowance handouts.

He's planning his finances early in life, because he knows he's the one responsible for his life. If he doesn't make it happen, no one will.

The argument for allowances is usually that kids need to learn how to manage money. But why not give them the opportunity, will, and desire to both make and manage it?

Whether in or out of the courtroom, I love observing ways we mothers can guide our children toward contributing well to society!

Lord Jesus, help us teach our children to give by giving back to the world when opportunities arise. Help us catch the vision of what one disciplined life can do. Help us teach them to give back to society by not handing them everything even when we want to.

Day 94

Do not be anxious about anything, but in everything by prayer and supplication with thanksgiving let your requests be made known to God.

And the peace of God, which surpasses all understanding, will guard your hearts and your minds in Christ Jesus. (Philippians 4:6–7, ESV)

"Mom, my cat has fleas!" she cried out.

I looked at her in disbelief. "What?!"

"Yes, we'll have to buy flea shampoo and take care of the whole house."

A few minutes later she cried out again, "Mooooom, I found one on my bed!"

My brain went into denial mode the way it always does when I'm hit with bug news, but the daughter, paranoid of anything jumping and hopping, is losing it much like her older sister did when she found lice one day.

Every other second there's another sound of distress until I see her curled up in her bed, refusing to move. "Can you get me a drink?" she asks.

I shake my head. "Child, you're going to have to get out of bed, use the toilet, get your own water, and simply live. Tomorrow we're going to take care of these fleas. Breathe."

Large brown eyes looked back at me nervously, but she obeyed. Before long she was out of her first state of paranoia and doing what it took to function even in a house infested with fleas from her beloved cat.

That cat was part of her heart and soul. We moved her from the West Coast to the East, paid for her to be in our rental, and snuggled her almost like she was a human. She'd given birth to nine litters of kittens which were sold for a hefty price, and had recently had her last two kittens before a scheduled surgery to end her reproductive phase.

My daughter bought her own iPhone with that kitten money. But even more important, she loved her cat for the cat's sake.

Her previous cat had been maimed and wounded after getting lost, but my daughter loved her fervently. She was just like that—bonded to her pets and people—so I did what I needed to do. PetSmart got one hundred dollars for flea chemicals the next day, and we sprayed, cleaned, and vacuumed all day long.

I don't even like house pets and have always said they're gross. But the cat was an opportunity to support my daughter, and now an opportunity to help her manage stress.

"If we freak out over smaller things, honey, we are constantly stressed and constantly projecting chaos into the atmosphere. The things to freak out over are larger things like hurricanes, death, or cancer. Tomorrow we will knock these fleas out of their bliss, and all will be well."

I hold her hands and pray, then encourage her again to *breathe.*

"We often can't take stressful things *out* of our lives," I keep saying. "But we can learn how to handle stressful things *in* our lives."

She knew what I was talking about. She'd watched her own mama be stressed plenty of times in the past years as we all faced betrayal, abandonment, divorce, a move across the country, and then, COVID-19.

I reached down to her sweet face and pulled her into a hug before leaving the room.

My head hit the pillow and I was thankful. Thankful that in a world of chaos over large and small things, there was still peace, still enough air to breathe, still enough for everything we needed even if we were lacking things we wanted.

Life can be used every single day, mothers. Walk with your child, empathize with your child, then lead your child to manage the stress of this world with the heart and peace of heaven.

Father, thank You that You lead us to peace. Because of You, we can lay our heads down at night and sleep in peace. You are our safe place, our shelter, and our help. Thank You for being our Father, and help us lead our children to the same peace.

DAY 95

"For I know the plans I have for you," declares the Lord, "plans for welfare and not for evil, to give you a future and a hope." (Jeremiah 29:11, ESV)

I'm waking the kids for Monday-morning school, and I'm scratching the same back I massaged last night. Those early morning back scratches are a great start to the day for some children.

Some kids feel loved by touch while others would rather hear affirming words.

I'm calling the other child and telling her she's beautiful in pink. I see a sleepy smile emerge on her face, and I realize this speaks love to her.

Some kids need lots of affirming words.

Being a mama in each season is tough work. If you've been faint-hearted before, you are certain to grow a spine through mothering.

Yesterday (and many days like it) found me home alone with two younger kids while the two older ones stayed out with friends. I had cooked a nice dinner, but not everyone was home to enjoy it together. A few weeks ago a mom of many teens told me she often doesn't know if there will be two at her dinner table or eight. And we don't get to throw a fit about it and refuse to cook. The two little ones need the same nutrients that you worked hard to prepare when everyone was home.

I pick up the older kids, and they're eating some sort of green-dyed, cold, creamy stuff right out of the container with plastic spoons.

I moan a little inside but shut my mama mouth and choose to feel thankful that they're safe and happy.

The orderly life I crave (and will never have) needs to be surrendered. Will my kids be drawn to a mama who's constantly trying to keep them in a tidy box of perfect schedules and meals and health?

They fill the kitchen once again and say, "I miss you, Mama."

The words are like music to a mama who loved the toddler days, having had three kids in a little over three years. I didn't really mind getting up at night with a tiny baby, and I loved having them around me 24/7.

The easiest, most blessed life with kids is surrendering to the seasons.

When they were small I was with them all the time. I loved it. My days were filled with walking to the park from our small apartment, doing chores alongside them, making hot chocolate for them when they came in from playing outdoors. I did my shopping with a cart full of kids and even breastfed my baby in the restroom of our grocery store. (I know, gross!) But babies squeal when they're hungry and they mess their diapers when they feel like it—not when it's handy.

Teens are a bit the same. In no season of life will a child think as much of Mama's needs and desires as they will of their own.

Mama has always been the hub of the wheel. Each spoke of the wheel sticks right into the hub, making it go round smoothly. Each season of their lives need to be connected to Mama to go round smoothly, but sometimes, *Mama needs to disconnect in order to connect.*

We don't really get to be kids anymore even when we want to be. There are days when I just want someone to realize I'm fully human and have human desires and I'm not just everyone's chauffeur, all the time.

I want them, still, to be like that. Playing and living and growing right beside me.

But rather than hold on to a season, I need to move with the flow so I can make the most of the next season.

I also need to go a step further and try to understand the cause and effect of my own life. And I know I can see my own gaping needs causing needs in them. Can I also own that to them, and ask for forgiveness?

I don't need to feel good about myself—I need to own the goodness of God, and he says that his goodness (his shame or his condemnation), leads us to repentance.

Do we see how good God is, and how his goodness isn't always shown in ways that make us feel good about our own lives or selves? His goodness leads us to see our need and make appropriate changes for the good of others.

To do what's good for your child, you may need to do what doesn't feel good for you.

To bring goodness to the heart of your child, you may need to ask your child to help you see that yuck in the heart of yourself.

To bring life, you may need to relinquish your own definition of that life, and be willing to adapt and change.

Mothers, can we be brave in each season, embrace each stage, and willingly let go? Because if our kids are our main source of joy, they will know it—and they will want Mama to find her own joy as they leave the nest and learn to fly.

Be wise, and make the most of your time with them. Be there, and then, be willing to back away a bit. Allow them to grow their wings, spread them, and fly.

They will always return, sooner or later, for that one thing only Mama can give—and that is *a mother's love.*

Father, thank You that our joy and identity is so much greater than being surrounded by those we love, even our own children. We are fully loved by You, all the time and in every way as we mother our children, then watch them go. Help us find Your life in all seasons.

Day 96

The steadfast love of the Lord never ceases; His mercies never come to an end; they are new every morning; great is Your faithfulness. (Lamentations 3:22–23, ESV)

I took a bite of salted caramel ice cream and handed the container back to my son.

The sun shone warmly down on us and the river rushed along below the railroad bridge. I'd forgotten how beautiful this place was.

I had also nearly forgotten what it was like to have my son smiling and opening his heart. Recently, he'd been quieter than he'd ever been—and he'd always been an open book, sweetheart kind of a guy, so my brain was reeling a little.

I had been tossing the idea of asking him if there's anything he needed to talk about—but I had already tried that and gotten only a growl, or a woof, or whatever you call that noise when a growing male wants to be left alone.

But today he was sharing his heart and asking about mine, and it felt wonderful. He had turned down a job or two so he could enjoy the sunny day out with Mama instead. We toured the dairy farm and bought ice cream, walked the bridge, and stopped by Walmart, where I loaded him up on clothes he needed.

That night, he came into my bedroom to say goodnight, sat on the bed, and began telling me about his music experience.

"Do you remember the days when I was so angry all the time?" he asked.

I nodded my head. Did I ever!

"Well," he confessed, "I had been listening to the wrong music during math. I'd turn on angry music when I felt angry, and it made me so much worse."

I didn't scold or rebuke at this point. Here was a vulnerable child voluntarily sharing his heart.

I listened, and I learned. "Maybe when I'm so mad, you can realize there are bigger issues going on," he said.

I nodded, again. Sure thing, son! Mama was well aware—for a long time—that there was probably a deeper issue.

But you can't force change until someone's ready, and you can't pressure peace onto others or it is no longer peace. A mother's heart needs to beat steady.

I never expected mothering to be this challenging even though everyone around assured me this was *normal*. And I'd think to myself, *well, then, I don't want normal.*

I loved the younger years, because life was steady. But as I see the contrast in my son (literally overnight), I'm reminded again not to take everything so personally.

Rather than take things personally, take them steadily. Slow your beating heart a little and breathe deep.

Your kids need to see a steady mama. One who prays each day. One who opens her Bible to teach and inspire each day. One who forgives readily and moves on easily.

They also need one who is strong enough not to base her worth on something as unsteady as her children. Mama, your child often doesn't feel steady and he needs you to be the steady.

If you haven't been a strong woman before, be one now.

Take the heat.

Refuse to absorb the attitude.

Don't allow yourself to drown in the drama.

Cry to the Lord when you want to cringe in front of them.

Learn to laugh it off a little more readily.

Be there.

Be willing to ask personal questions, or wait to ask anything because you're tuning in with wisdom rather than emotion.

And always, always talk about the hard stuff. There is no topic off limits with your child. Pursue the deep things many parents avoid, and do it on purpose.

Not every day will be as peaceful with this son as yesterday was. Today might be rocky again—who knows?

But my heart will beat steady—because God knows and he asks us mothers to know His peace more than we know anything else.

Jesus, thank You that You show Yourself so strong when we don't know what the answers are. Thank You for loving us steadily when our days are no longer as steady as they used to be. Help us show our children Your faithfulness by being there with the same love and care we've always had for them.

DAY 97

For by grace you have been saved through faith. And this is not your own doing; it is the gift of God, not as a result of works, so that no one may boast. (Ephesians 2:8–9, ESV)

"You are so beautiful!" I tell my daughters often.

They look back at me and say, "Of course you think so—you're our *mom*."

I smile and know I am unbiased in my view of them, my two daughters whom I love with my heart and soul.

I want them to enjoy all things good, be secure in who they are, know what it's like to be loved and appreciated. So, I praise them—and rightly so—until I realize I also need to be careful what I praise them for and how I do it.

I praise them for getting good grades and for doing a good job scrubbing that bathroom. I compliment them when they're good with people and make new friends. But then, I pause.

Their sense of being loved and appreciated needs to go so much deeper than performance. If I only praise them when they accomplish something noteworthy, what am I teaching them?

I'm the mom who used to be the all-time people pleaser, performing to exhaustion so I could be loved and approved of. Those surrounding me didn't always know that because they were silent when I needed them but praised me when I served them, I was developing an almost desperate desire to be what people wanted me to be, all so I could experience the love I craved.

I'd stare in amazement at women who were OK with disapproval. I couldn't relate to the peace they felt even when others weren't happy with them. *I based my internal sense of well-being on the external approval of others—and found myself on a very shaky foundation.*

Thank God, I learned sooner or later that my foundation is the unshakable love of Jesus Christ, that no matter what, I could run to Him for all the love I needed and for exorbitant amounts of grace. He was my safe place, my anchor, my Lover.

I began to create a safe place for my children even when they messed up.

I gave them grace when they broke a dish and spilled milk all over the floor. "Accidents happen to all of us," became my mantra.

I wanted my children to feel safe with me when they did something that many adults would be angry over.

I wanted my children to be as safe with me as I was with Jesus Christ.

Along with that came an intense desire to let my child know that he or she was approved of and loved even if the report card came back with lower grades than I wanted.

What mattered was their effort, not their performance.

If you praise only performance, you soon create a child who will perform, then look around to see who notices. What you want is a child who happily and securely does life without worrying about who notices.

Our often-naive efforts can produce adults who don't know how to live without others' approval. Complimenting effort more than performance, and giving grace during mistakes, releases them from the need to perform for praise and approval as adults.

"I love how hard you tried," I tell my daughter as she groans over her less-than-perfect artwork. "You'll only improve as time goes by. Nothing can be perfect from the start."

"It's OK," I tell my exceptionally perfectionistic son as glass shatters across the kitchen floor and milk runs madly to all forbidden corners where it threatens to sit and rot. "Accidents happen to all of us. Mama is not angry."

He's the child who helps me clean up pools of water from a washer that's overflowing across the kitchen floor. Towel after waterlogged towel gets dragged willingly outside by this boy because he loves order and he loves his mama.

I have to be extra careful with this one. Already he's distraught over messy things, mistakes, and less-than-perfect scenarios of any kind. He's a perfectionist like I've never seen in a boy. It's up to me to help him breathe easy, even—and especially when—he's the one creating the mess.

Rather than tense up with a mistake, ease up with it. Why expect a child to be perfect in such a fragmented world? When we quickly criticize each mistake, this is what we portray—*you shouldn't make mistakes.*

Every child needs to know there's room for growth and that it's OK not to be the best in the room.

Every adult needs to live in humility and kindness to others rather than that eager "please notice me" attitude that's so obnoxious to others.

The mother who only rewards her son when he wins that baseball game doesn't know that she's creating a future show-off rather than a man who will live his fullest without needing constant praise.

But, the mother who stops for ice cream and encouragement for his efforts after he loses the game instills a deep sense of true value and security in her child.

"Mother loves me, she loves me, she loves me. Mother loves me more than my performance. I don't have to perform to be loved by my mother."

A subconscious awareness of true value begins to bud in this child's mind. Remember always, mothers—*we teach most by the subliminal advocacy of our own lives.*

Tell your daughters they're beautiful, cheer for your son's winning game—but don't stop there. Cheer them on for their efforts, too. Create a safe place for them to fail. Let them know they can relax and breathe and live.

Father, thank You so much for being my safe place. It's what drew me to You, what let me know You are who You say You are. Your goodness led me to You, and Your patience keeps me with You. Help me mother my children in this very way.

Day 98

Look carefully then how you walk, not as unwise but as wise, making the best use of the time. (Ephesians 5: 15&16)

Sometimes practical wisdom fosters spiritual peace. Our homes are the most important places for us to learn time management and skill because this brings beauty, order, and peace.

My mother was the best at turning ancient ugly spaces into clean, welcoming havens. This doesn't take a lot of money; it takes self-discipline and time management skills.

Homes should be havens. The following tips on scheduling are things I learned by watching my mother, and anyone can implement them by tweaking them to fit their specific needs.

Nothing has helped me more than routine and schedule. I love knowing what to do when it's time to do it, rather than winging each day as it comes and hoping things get done.

Schedules are guidelines, helpers, stay-on-taskers. They are not masters. My schedule changes through the years and there are times when the routine is much less stringent than other times.

Keep a light approach to a schedule while at the same time implementing it daily whenever possible. This ensures the kids' Bible time, makes sure the dishwasher is unloaded before the next child needs to load it, and releases us from the frustration of always having a crummy bathroom or piles of laundry.

A schedule also ensures that the most important things of a day get done. I schedule reading to my children, which means when evening comes, I know it's time to pick up the Bible and call them together even when I'm tired and would rather hang out on my phone. Making a schedule based on what your children need for a lifetime rather than what you feel like doing in a moment is so important!

For me, schedule spells freedom and peace. I used to run about without getting my own self ready and prepped for the day—now, quiet time simply happens quietly and I know when to fold up the laptop and head for the mirror. I don't stare in the mirror when half the day is over and wonder at the scarecrow I see, because that face was cared for as one of the first tasks of my day.

I know when to wipe the breakfast table rather than stare at crumb-covered tabletops all morning.

A good schedule is one that keeps you on track, but doesn't master you. If it's Thursday night and your older kids want to stay out for Dairy Queen with their friends, you can allow them as long as they still rise for school on time the next morning.

They can rise, exhausted, and eat cold pizza for breakfast from the night before. There can be dishes on the counter for twenty-four hours without you feeling like a loser—because good moms are moms who can allow dirty dishes at times without losing their sanity.

Bend a little, then get right back on track. Allow your kids to grow up with the benefit of knowing how to master their time and make it productive, but not be so rigid that the very air they breathe is stifled.

Lord Jesus, help us to turn our houses into homes where order and peace is a soothing atmosphere for our families in a chaotic world.

DAY 99

For you were called to freedom, brothers. Only do not use your freedom as an opportunity to the flesh, but through love serve one another. (Galatians 5:13, ESV)

One of my children is a great leader and could probably become politician or attorney if she wanted to.

One of them is a giver and loves to bless others by sharing and serving.

One of them is a mercy person and has others coming to him for help and comfort.

One is a detailed perfectionist with a goal to have his first car be a Lamborghini. In all reality, he'll probably end up with the best job and he has at least one sibling hoping to gain from his future monetary excess.

"I'll take my Lamborghini to all the thrift stores," he says. I smile at the mental picture as I visualize him doing exactly what he said.

Mama raised him to be frugal and shop for clothes at thrift stores. At nine years old he knows all too well what it means to be patient as his teen sisters roam thrift store aisles for an hour, then spend another hour in the dressing rooms before emerging with one or two items that actually worked.

It's enough to make a little boy start darting between the clothes racks and peeking out for a wished-for game of hide-and-seek. He may or may not get a laugh from his mama, but at any rate he's tickling my sides and crashing into me on purpose as he tries hard not to go completely nuts.

Girl shopping can make little boys go absolutely bonkers. But, he's already convinced that thrifting is the way to save money—especially if he's paying off his dream car!

I take the opportunity to help the boys give to the girls even if they don't understand. I want to raise understanding adults, and that won't happen if Little Buddy hears me pressure the girls to hurry every time he complains or tickles my arm one more time in the clothing aisle.

"Girls just take a while to shop," I tell him. "Someday your wife will take a long time, too, and you'll be such a great man to give her the space she needs."

Showing your children how to accept and give to each other is a key element to mothering well.

Acceptance changes the atmosphere to a safe place of peace. And as a mother, I can do the same thing as I celebrate my children's strong points rather than focus on the weak ones.

I sent my one child a note the other day, "Remember that your strength is a gift. Lead by principle to be a great leader."

I threw in the encouragement because children need to know that even as we train them to be what they need to be, we also celebrate who they already are. I can celebrate my child's strength even as I fine-tune her leadership.

I can accept that my giving child won't lead as well as the strong child, and that my strong child won't serve as instinctively as the giving child.

What's more, I can accept their unique struggles just as I accept their unique strengths. I can and should expect them to have needs as I simply observe and seek wisdom on how to lead them to better things.

Mothers, we often do an internal panic over a seen need. As if our children are already angels, we struggle to come to grips with blatant character flaws and spend our days worrying them away. Our constant fear and criticism does the exact opposite of what we want. We correct flaws, scold, and give consequences more than we celebrate goodness, encourage, and lead by example.

I want us to adjust our mindset from one of fear to one of calmly standing on the sidelines, *expecting issues to rise.*

I want us to be the steady faithfulness our children can depend on when their own emotions take them to shaky places.

I want us to stay calm in the face of struggle and reach out to appropriate sources for answers and help.

I want our children to see us utterly humble and willing to make adjustments if what we're doing isn't working.

I want us to have a warrior mindset rather than a tourist mentality. Warriors head across the seas prepared for and expecting difficulty. Tourists travel to other lands preparing for nothing but ease. When difficulties arise, they are devastated, shocked, and panicky rather than prepared.

Mothers, we need to let go of the inner need to perfect our children in one day. It's OK if the day goes a little sideways and everyone heads to bed hoping for a better one tomorrow. The larger picture here is one of struggle and growth, growth and struggle, as we all gain momentum toward the goal.

I expect my strong child to struggle with kindness.

I expect my mercy child to struggle with laziness.

I expect my giving child to struggle with depression.

I expect my perfectionist to struggle with crankiness when something doesn't line up perfectly.

By expecting it, I don't mean accepting it. I'm talking about taking it with grace, realizing that if I as an adult have needs, my children certainly do too. This inner shift changes me from despair over a bad day to one of peace at the end of that same day.

I can keep kingdom solutions in mind as I face human opposition. My children need me to be this for them.

At the end of the day, I celebrate each child and call out the good even as I address each need and strive to lead them to better things.

Cheers, mothers! We are warriors, not tourists—and our weapons are praise, peace, and bringing the goodness of God into each life of those we love.

Lord Jesus, thank You that Your standard of love is service to each other in spite of imperfections. Thank You for walking with us closely. Help us do the same for each other.

Day 100

Surely goodness and mercy shall follow me all the days of my life. (Psalm 23:6, ESV)

"You don't know what you're talking about," one child said to the other.

There was a moment of silence on the back seat before she tried again to express what she wanted to say.

"You're not a teenager yet and you have no idea what you're even talking about," the other child repeated. "Why do you always try to be bigger than you are?"

The atmosphere in the car tensed up a bit as I struggled to know what to say. "Please don't talk to her like that," I said. "There is no need to put her down."

"I'm not putting her down," said the child. "I'm just telling her what she's doing."

Then, "You're so sensitive, Mom."

He's right—I am sensitive. But I've come to celebrate that fact because being sensitive allows me to empathize deeply with others. I can feel their feelings almost as if they're my own. I care deeply for others and want everyone to be encouraged. And I try to lead my children into kinder ways of communicating.

Did you know that most of the time you can say what you need to say without being a slap in the face or a grinding halt to the joy of another's soul? The child who put the other child down could have simply said, "Hey, this is really how it works. Do you want me to explain it to you?" There was no need to tell her she was always trying to "be bigger than she was," or she "had no idea what she was talking about."

One method tears down, creates sadness and even anxiety, and makes someone stop in their tracks before trying again to express themselves. Even more, this method sheds no light on what the truth really is. All it does is tear down and strip joy while depriving another of the information they don't have.

This is not Jesus's way, and us mothers need to notice these things and teach a better way.

I know what it's like to be nervous and on edge because of constant criticism. I know what it's like to perform less and less well because I was always prepping for the next correction.

Then, I know what it's like to be surrounded with so much encouragement that all the best parts of my life come alive. I know what it's like to breathe without fear. To put forth my best efforts, knowing that even if I mess up I'll be met with love and encouragement.

I've seen children live in families where every little and big thing is corrected and scolded. I've seen them develop fear and nervousness rather than confidence and ease. My heart breaks for these children. Mothers do this unawares, many times.

When your son cooks dinner for the family (or even for himself), can you walk into the kitchen and see about ten different things he could have done differently, but bite your tongue and thank him sincerely for his efforts?

It's said that for one criticism, people need one hundred encouraging comments.

When your daughter does the laundry, can you notice her efforts and verbalize your appreciation without scolding her for forgetting that one last load that was left in the washer overnight and now needs a second run through?

Our children learn as they go and there are one million reasons for criticism each day because they haven't been doing things for forty years. Our tendency to overcorrect can sap the life right out of them.

Some mothers focus on praise before criticism. Even though they're encouraging first, they criticize all the time. Their child learns to expect a criticism as soon as the praise is over. This undoes everything the encouragement was meant to accomplish, and continues to create a sense of never being good enough.

We don't realize the long-term effects on a child who never feels good enough. As they grow older, this can transfer into giving in to peer pressure to a crowd who tells them they won't fit in or be part of a group unless they do certain things.

A major drug problem can begin simply with a child wanting to finally feel OK and "good enough" for a group of people.

Mothers, the way we parent affects society. Does your child live in emotional safety, or is he always on edge, afraid of how he's going to mess up next?

My children didn't understand why I focused so hard on lessening criticism in our home. I had tasted both kinds of living and I knew which one I wanted for my home.

An atmosphere of life happens when you speak out life-giving words more than draining words. For heaven's sake, we mothers can imperfect the very people we try so hard to perfect, all the while having no idea what we're doing.

The daughter who left the last load of laundry in the washer can simply be told, "Hey, there's one load left. I'll run the washer again so it doesn't smell, but next time try to check on the last load. Thank you so much for doing the laundry!"

That method teaches her to be more aware while at the same time showing her encouragement. You're willing to run the load again because you're not angry, and she can tell. You're also being a responsible mother by teaching her to be aware next time. If she continues to forget, there will be time for a lesson.

Many of our criticisms are not lessons to drive home; they are chances for mothers to jump on imperfections and make big deals out of them because their own hearts are not at rest.

There are much greater things to be angry or even critical over. When or if the time comes where you need to handle those things, you'll be so thankful for everything you said that established your love for, and acceptance of, your child.

As with my children in the car, take every opportunity to show them how to be honest but do it honorably. There is never a need to push another down just because you feel a need to express your own thoughts. Then, take it a step further and help them allow the other to fail, mispronounce a word, or say something without pouncing on every single "wrong" move.

Emotional safety is our goal more than being intellectually correct is our goal.

Father, help our words to be as gold to those around us. When we need to correct someone, help us do it in the kindest way possible. Help us to live and speak with both conviction and compassion.

Notes

Notes

Notes

....

....

....

....

....

....

....

....

....

....

....

....

....

....

....

....

....

Notes

....

....

....

....

....

....

....

....

....

....

....

....

....

....

....

....

....

Notes

....

....

....

....

....

....

....

....

....

....

....

....

....

....

....

....

Notes

....

....

....

....

....

....

....

....

....

....

....

....

....

....

....

....

....

....

Notes

Notes

Notes

....

....

....

....

....

....

....

....

....

....

....

....

....

....

....

....

....

....

Notes

_____

_____

_____

_____

_____

_____

_____

_____

_____

_____

_____

_____

_____

_____

_____

_____

Notes

....

....

....

....

....

....

....

....

....

....

....

....

....

....

....

....

....

....

ALSO AVAILABLE

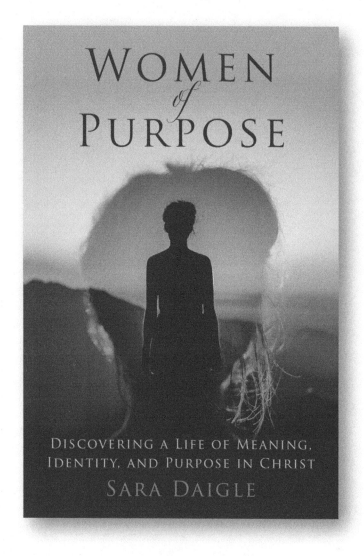

WOMEN
of
PURPOSE

DISCOVERING A LIFE OF MEANING,
IDENTITY, AND PURPOSE IN CHRIST
SARA DAIGLE

www.goodbooks.com